IMAGES
of America

GHOST TOWNS
OF DEATH VALLEY

Many of the ghost towns of the Death Valley area can be found on this Tonopah & Tidewater Railroad route map. Starting from the west, at Owens Lake, are the towns of Darwin, Coso, Lookout, Modock, and Millspaugh. In the north are Rhyolite, Bullfrog, Chloride Cliff, Keane Wonder, Lees (Lee), Skidoo, Harrisburg, Wild Rose, and Furnace Ranch. Farther south are Ryan, Death Valley Junction, Evelyn, Greenwater, Keys Camp, Zabriskie, and Ibex. (Courtesy of the Robert P. Palazzo Collection.)

ON THE COVER: One of Hungry Bill's sons stands in the middle of Main Street in Darwin. Jack Gunn's saloon is in the background. Hungry Bill was best known for having made raids into San Bernardino and Los Angeles with his brother Panamint Tom in the 1870s, stealing horses from the ranches. (Courtesy of the Robert P. Palazzo Collection.)

IMAGES
of America

GHOST TOWNS
OF DEATH VALLEY

Robert P. Palazzo

ARCADIA
PUBLISHING

Published by Arcadia Publishing
Charleston, South Carolina

Library of Congress Control Number: 2014933922

For all general information, please contact Arcadia Publishing:
Telephone 843-853-2070
Fax 843-853-0044
E-mail sales@arcadiapublishing.com
For customer service and orders:
Toll-Free 1-888-313-2665

Visit us on the Internet at www.arcadiapublishing.com

This book is dedicated to Joseph Paolo Palazzo, whose lifelong passion for ghost towns is unsurpassed and who provided constant inspiration for this work, and to my wife, Vivianne, who has cheerfully endured Death Valley the place and all my Death Valley books.

CONTENTS

ACKNOWLEDGMENTS

I would like to thank the following individuals, who provided encouragement, support, and/or help during the course of this project: Dale Alberstone, Thomas A. Baier, Chuck Champion, the curators and staff of Death Valley National Park Museum, Michael Dawson, John DeSimio, Katherine Duggan, Ted Faye, Judge Christopher Frisco, Rick Gibson, Dana Gioia, Henry Golas, the curators and staff of the Eastern California Museum, Michael Hecht, Reginald Hill, Eric James, Charles "O'C" Johnson, Gregory Krisilas, Denny Kruska, Jim Lorenzo, Stan McClain, Donald J. Palazzo, Chuck Rennie, James E. Smith, Laura Stalker and the staff of the Huntington Library, the late Hugh Tolford and his daughter Katherine, Will Townsend, and, last but certainly not least, Robert Varlotta. I also want to thank "T" and "J," who wish to remain anonymous, but they know who they are. In addition, my editor, Jared Nelson, has provided advice and help. Of course, I am indebted to my wife, Vivianne, who once again had to endure the long and time-consuming process of book authorship, but who did so with a smile and who continued to offer valuable suggestions and insights.

The following photograph sources are credited with abbreviations or a name: Palm Springs Art Museum, Stephen H. Willard Photography Collection & Archive (Willard); National Park Service, Death Valley National Park (NPS); photographs taken by Frank Green and courtesy of W.C. Hendrick (FG); photographs taken by and courtesy of Tom Murray (Murray); Eastern California Museum (ECM). All other photographs are courtesy of the Robert P. Palazzo Collection.

INTRODUCTION

Death Valley National Park encompasses an area of about 3.4 million acres. It is a land of extremes, with altitudes ranging from 11,049 feet at the snowy summit of Telescope Peak in the Panamint Range to the depths of Badwater Basin at 282 feet below sea level, the lowest point on the North American continent. In fact, both the highest and lowest points in the contiguous United States can be seen on a clear day at Dante's View. The highest temperature ever recorded on Earth was 134 degrees, near where the Furnace Creek Inn now stands. Given these extremes, and as the very name "Death Valley" suggests, death can be ever-present. This imagery of death extends not only to people and other living things but to its towns as well.

While there is no consensus as to the definition of a ghost town, pioneer ghost town author Lambert Florin probably said it best when he described a ghost town as a town that is "a shadowy semblance of a former self." Although the Death Valley area is sparsely populated, it has been the home of a surprising number of towns, many of which have disappeared not only from the desert but also from history. Some are known only because they applied for and received a post office charter from the US government, while others are remembered as stops on the railroads that initially served Death Valley's mining companies and, later, its tourists before becoming ghosts themselves. Although many of these towns have left a small though tangible reminder of their existence, some have left nothing but memories. One such town, Camp Dawson, was an elaborate mining scam promotion and existed only in the mind of its creator, I.X. Dawson. Today, some of these towns still barely hang on to their existence, such as Ballarat, Darwin, and Death Valley Junction. Others, like Shoshone and Tecopa, though small, are a little more secure and would not be considered a "ghost" or a "semi-ghost." Beatty, Nevada, established in 1905 as a supply town, later became a railroad hub. Although the railroads are gone, the town, on US Highway 95 between Tonopah and Las Vegas, is in no imminent danger of disappearing and becoming a ghost.

Towns were established in the Death Valley region during three main periods. The first were the result of boomtowns that were formed due to mining excitements in the 1870s. Ghost towns established at this time were Cerro Gordo, Darwin, Kasson, Panamint, Reilly, and Tecopa. The next period of mining activity was during the 1890s, and it spawned the creation of post offices in Argus, Ballarat, Modock, and Millspaugh. Modock was the location of the 1870s mining town of Lookout, but a post office was never established at Lookout due to its proximity and economic connection to Darwin. Millspaugh actually got its post office in 1902.

The most prolific era when post offices were established in the Death Valley region was during the boom period of 1906–1907, fueled primarily by the high price of copper. Post offices that were established during these two years were Alkali, Death Valley (originally located at what is now Death Valley Junction), Donald, Furnace, Goldvalley, Greenwater, Hoveck, Keane Springs, Lee, Neptune, Ryan, Schwab, Skidoo, and Zabriskie. Most of these post offices were in business for only a year or two, closing after the market crashed and their populations fled. Many of these

1906–1907 post offices existed only on paper. The townsite's promoters (who were also mining promoters) would petition Washington for a post office, giving a glowing report of the area and the estimated population—both fictional. When the post office examiners ultimately determined that the town did not warrant having a post office, the official post office would be rescinded without there having been any postal activity, or even a town at all, for that matter. Examples include Alakali, Donald, Furnace, Goldvalley, Keane Springs, and Neptune.

Thereafter, post offices were established sporadically for a variety of reasons. Keane Wonder was granted a post office in 1912 to serve the mining center that grew around the Keane Wonder mine. Leadfield obtained a post office in 1926 for the town that was created to promote a mining swindle. Both Panamint Springs in 1940 and Scotty's Castle in 1947 were given post offices to serve the tourists who were visiting and staying in the area. Both of these facilities were fairly short lived, with Panamint Springs closing in 1946 and Scotty's Castle in 1953.

While most of the towns that were located in the Death Valley area are no longer viable and are forgotten ghosts, their impact survives to this day. The mines of the Death Valley region's mining districts, and the towns that were created as a result of the economic activity of those mines, were instrumental in founding the Southern California towns of Santa Monica and Inglewood. They provided the stimulus and capital for Los Angeles's first boom period, enabling it to grow from a sleepy pueblo into a city. Reminders of this legacy can be found today in street names in the Los Angeles area. Gone are the Nadeau Hotel, Nadeau Block, and Nadeau Station, but there is still Beaudry in downtown Los Angeles, named for Prudent Beaudry, a mayor of Los Angeles who was the partner of his brother Victor, the water king of Cerro Gordo, Darwin and the New Coso District. Bicknell Street in Santa Monica is named for prominent Panamint and Darwin doctor F.T. Bicknell. And while it seems odd that two streets in Santa Monica (Jones Street and Stewart Street) are named after two senators from Nevada, the fact that their ownership of the Panamint mines led to the development of Santa Monica more than justifies it.

One

PANAMINT AND BALLARAT

Mining in the area near Panamint actually started in December 1860, when Dr. Samuel G. George and William Henderson found a silver-bearing lode about three miles southeast of Wildrose Spring. They organized the Telescope Mining District in the spring of 1861, and mining activity was carried on by the Combination Gold & Silver Mining Co. until 1863, when Panamint Indians killed four of the miners and burned the camp.

The traditional discovery of the mines near Panamint was made in December 1872 by Robert P. Stewart, William M. Kennedy, and Richard C. Jacobs. This discovery gave rise to the founding of the town of Panamint and led to a supply center in Los Angeles, a new port, and a railroad terminus, Santa Monica. Although the capital for developing the Panamint mines came from San Francisco, the City of Los Angeles was the beneficiary. The expected trade from the mines in Panamint was sufficient for the Los Angeles Chamber of Commerce, in its first official act, to put up the money for the Panamint Wagon Road so that the trade would come to the city.

Panamint was the only Inyo County mining camp that had its own bank, the Bank of Panamint. However, the Surprise Valley Mining & Water Co., by far Panamint's largest mining and business entity, did its banking with Harris Newmark & Co. of Los Angeles. The total production from Panamint was very limited (estimated at only $70,000), but it had the most hype, the most influential backers, and a colorful, though brief, history.

The town of Ballarat was founded in 1896 as a supply station for miners in the area. It thrived during the period of Death Valley's revived mining excitement, and by 1905, Ballarat had a population estimated as between 400 and 500 residents. It hosted seven saloons, three hotels, a Wells Fargo office, and a school. Ballarat's post office was established in 1897 and survived until 1917.

This is Main Street in Panamint City in 1872, shortly after the town's founding. The stamp mill with the millworks and buildings can be seen at the end of town, at the foot of Surprise Canyon. Different types of construction are in evidence: stone buildings with wood roofs; wooden buildings, some with false fronts; canvas tent cabins; and brick construction. (NPS.)

George Hansen was a Panamint Indian who, in 1861, led Dr. Samuel George up Surprise Canyon, just missing locating the rich Panamint lodes. Though Dr. George was the first to achieve success in the Panamints at Wildrose, he did not trust "Indian George," so he turned back before the big strike at Panamint. Dr. George returned in 1874 to find all the good deposits already taken.

Panamint's newspaper, the *Panamint News*, was published by Civil War veteran T.S. Harris. When Panamint's boom ended, Harris moved the entire printing press and newspaper operations to the new mining boomtown of Darwin and established the *Coso Mining News*, printing its first issue on November 6, 1875. When Darwin's boom ended in 1878, he again moved the entire printing press and newspaper to Bodie and renamed the paper the *Bodie Standard*.

113. Freighting t Panamint.

The caption "Freighting to Panamint" describes this scene of a pack train getting ready to head to the new mining boomtown of Panamint from Los Angeles. Death Valley was isolated from major supply centers, so materials had to be imported from great distances in order to build houses, mills, stores, and even towns that boasted populations of thousands of people.

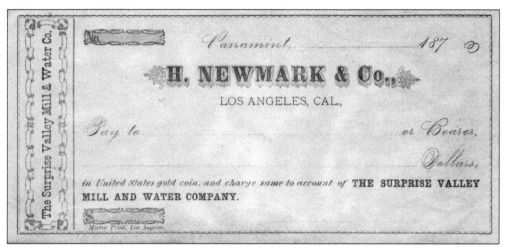

There was a close relationship between Panamint and Los Angeles, as this check indicates. The Surprise Valley Mill & Water Company was Panamint's largest enterprise. Owned by Nevada senators John P. Jones and William M. Stewart, it did its banking with H. Newmark & Co., the pioneer banking company in Los Angeles.

This 1874 photograph shows the substantial complex of Surprise Valley Mining Company, which comprised a mill, works, and buildings. The iconic large brick stack, which was partly standing in the 1990s, is prominent in the works; the two shorter chimneys to the left have long since disappeared. (Photograph by Jack Spaulding.)

In lieu of a Wells Fargo office, the Panamint Pony Express was used to carry mail from Panamint City to San Bernardino, with a stop in Darwin. The express operated in 1874 and 1875 and was owned and operated by Panamint's largest employer, the Surprise Valley Mining Company. The only known rider was Philip Ross. (Courtesy of Robert Varlotta.)

Despite having two banks, there was no Wells Fargo office. Panamint was located in a canyon, and there was a high danger of robbery. Senator Stewart solved the problem for transporting the silver to the mint in Carson City by casting it into "cannon balls" weighing hundreds of pounds, which were then loaded onto open wagons and sent without an armed guard to the mint.

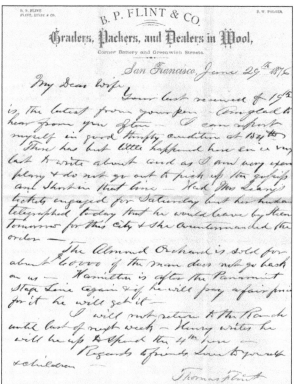

In this June 1876 letter, Thomas Flint, the owner of California's The Coast Line Stage Company, writes to his wife and declares that "Hamilton is after Panamint Stage Line again & if he will pay a fair price for it he will get it." William Hamilton ultimately did buy the Bakersfield, Lone Pine & Panamint Stage line from William Buckley in early 1877.

Panamint City was the first substantial town built in the Death Valley region. The Surprise Valley Mining Company mill, shown here in the early 20th century, was owned by senators John P. Jones and William F. Stewart. It operated around the clock, processing about 15 tons of ore per day.

This photograph of Main Street in Panamint City, taken near the large chimney stack of the Surprise Valley mill, looks down into the town. The words "Pilgrim Iron Works Los Angeles Cal" are visible on the mill machinery in the foreground. All of the heavy industrial mill equipment and building materials had to travel on the narrow twisting road up to the town, most of it from Los Angeles.

US senator William Morris Stewart played a prominent role in two of Death Valley's ghost towns. In the 1870s, he was the cofounder, with Sen. John J. Jones, and promoter of Panamint. At the turn of the 20th century, he moved to Bullfrog and maintained a law office there as well.

The Inyo Consolidated Mining Company was formed by George M. Pinney to cash in from Wall Street investors by promoting the Panamint Mill, originally owned by Sen. John Jones. When the company was reorganized as the Surprise Mining and Milling Company, Nelson G. Fairman, who signed this certificate as company secretary, built a new prefabricated mill in Panamint.

There is a widely held misconception that Panamint City was destroyed in a flood in July 1876. This is not true. Panamint's post office was still doing a brisk business in 1877, and the records for the Surprise Valley Mill and Water Company show significant activity that year. The mill shown here did suffer damage from a major fire, which ultimately led to Panamint's demise.

16

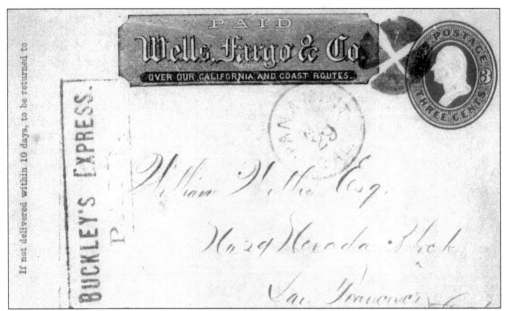

Although Panamint did not have a Wells Fargo office, it did have a US Post Office and utilized private companies, such as Buckley's Express, to carry the mail and provide express services. In addition to letters, these private express companies also carried packages and passengers. Here, Buckley's repurposed a Wells Fargo prepaid envelope, stamping its own name on it. (Courtesy of Bill Tatham.)

Indian George Hansen (left) and Shorty Harris were pioneers of early Death Valley and one-time inhabitants of its ghost towns. Indian George described early Ballarat: "Many men come, town spring up overnight, stage wagons, freight wagons come go all the time. Many saloons, much firewater, lots of fighting. Good place for Indian to stay away from."

Indian George Hansen claimed to be over 105 years old near the time of his death. Shown here reading (or at least holding) the February 1940 issue of *Desert* magazine, he told stories of his childhood, when he watched with awe the sight of the strange, bearded white men (the forty-niners). They were the first such men to enter Death Valley.

The Panamint Mountain Mines Syndicate was one of hundreds of mining companies formed in the Death Valley region during 1906 and 1907 to capitalize on the speculative frenzy. It was during this time that Bullfrog and Greenwater were formed. This company tried to exploit the name of the old mining camp of Panamint in order to add credibility to its gold claims in the Wild Rose District.

Ballarat was founded in 1896 to supply the mines in the canyons of the Panamint mountains during a revival of mining in the Panamint District. The town was the center for miners' activities in the area. Ballarat flourished in the first decade of the 20th century until its ultimate decline in 1917.

Frank "Shorty" Harris was one of the prominent residents of Ballarat. He prospected in both Tombstone and Death Valley after having worked underground in the Darwin mines in the 1870s. He is credited with the codiscovery of Bullfrog in Nevada (with Ed Cross) and Harrisburg in Death Valley.

Another famous Ballarat resident was Michael J. "Jim" Sherlock, who was always secretive about his past. Said to have been a gambler and gunfighter in Montana and Wyoming, Sherlock was best known for outwitting local gamblers in 1903 by driving a buggy with a team of burros to beat the speed record from Ballarat to Los Angeles previously set by a team of fast horses.

Ballarat denizens Shorty Harris (left) and Jim Sherlock were close friends, and they spent quite a bit of their last days together in Ballarat. Harris died in 1934, and Sherlock died in 1935. They are shown deep in discussion in front of the house they shared in Ballarat.

Shorty Harris (right) and Jim Sherlock stand in front of a car in Ballarat. The adobe house at left is slowly melting back into the desert, and the wood frame house in the right background is faring little better. The photograph is captioned "Shorty Harris and Jim Sherlock watch over the destiny of Ballarat, a ghost town which they hope will 'come back' some day."

Jim Sherlock was buried in the "Boot Hill" cemetery at Ballarat in 1935. He has the distinction of having the only marble gravestone in Ballarat's cemetery. After his death, rumors circulated that he had lived under an assumed name because of his mysterious past and that he seemed to have money without ever doing much work.

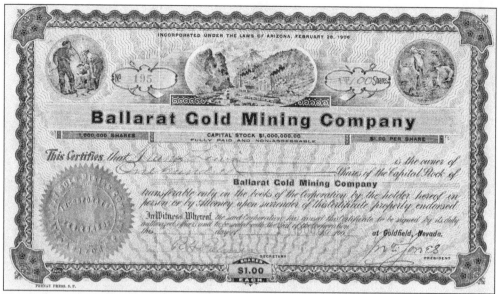

The Ballarat Gold Mining Company was another of the hundreds of companies formed in Death Valley in the first decade of the 20th century. Its president was John "January" Jones, a colorful character involved in the development of the mining boomtowns of Tonopah, Goldfield, Bullfrog, and Panamint. He was known to carry his gun openly, and he had a reputation as a gunfighter who was said to have killed more than one man in a gunfight.

Charles Ferge, better known as Seldom Seen Slim, is shown here with his corncob pipe. Slim was a popular "desert rat" and long a favorite with Death Valley visitors. He was in the later wave of Death Valley prospectors, arriving in Ballarat about 1912 and remaining a fixture there until his death in 1968.

Shorty Harris sits on a wooden bench on the main commercial street in Ballarat. The photograph bears the caption "In the 1930's, Shorty Harris held court at the old supply camp of Ballarat where he shared the limelight with Seldom Seen Slim. The faint outlines of his autograph 'Shorty Harris' appear just above his shoes."

Shorty Harris, at the center of this photograph, stands in front of a store in Ballarat with three unidentified men. The store is constructed with the typical adobe walls, a primary building feature in many of the structures in Ballarat.

Shorty Harris (second from right) sits on a chair in front of the old schoolhouse in Ballarat in January 1931. The school was no longer in use at this late date. The bearded man sitting on the ground next to Shorty is Ralph "Dad" Fairbanks, formerly of Greenwater and the founder of Shoshone. (Photograph by Merrill H. Deal.)

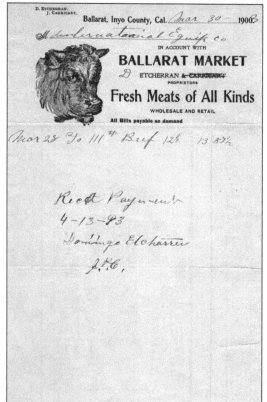

Domingo Etcharren, "the one-eyed Basque," was a butcher in Ballarat. Initially, he was in partnership with Jean Carricart. But by 1903, the date on this receipt, Carricart's name has been crossed out. Curiously, he signed the receipt for Etcharren. After Etcharren codiscovered the Keane Wonder mine in Death Valley, he used proceeds from its sale to establish a larger general merchandise store in Darwin.

The townsite of Shadow Mountain was founded in 1907 by Clarence E. Eddy, "The Poet-Prospector." Eddy claimed to have made a rich discovery in Johnson Canyon, on the opposite side of the mountain from old Panamint and below the east slope of Telescope Peak. A number of gullible prospectors followed Eddy, located a number of gold claims, and set up the camp.

Chris Wicht's saloon in Ballarat operated from 1902, when Wicht arrived, until 1917. During its heyday, the saloon was the focal point of all social activity in Ballarat. It claimed to have the only billiards table for miles around. Wicht was said to have found the table in the ruins at Panamint City, disassembled it, and carried it down Surprise Canyon, past his camp, and to his saloon.

Mining was central to the existence of most of the ghost towns of Death Valley. Shorty Harris, one of Death Valley's preeminent prospectors, is shown here sitting in front of his crumbling adobe house in Ballarat. Using a frying pan, Harris is "sampling a small quantity of ore that has been ground in a pestle."

As the last resident of Ballarat, Seldom Seen Slim liked to tell people that he voted himself mayor, postmaster, chief of police, dog catcher, and tax collector. In fact, the US government closed the post office at Ballarat on September 29, 1917, and, as an incorporated city, Ballarat would not have had a mayor.

Though known as a single-blanket prospector, Seldom Seen Slim stands proudly next to his jeep, which replaced his burros. The prospectors of Death Valley were slow to adjust with the times, but by the 1950s, even those most resistant to change adopted modern methods.

In an attempt to breathe some life into the dying town, a Ballarat Days Celebration was held in November 1965. Years of hard living in the harsh Death Valley environment took their toll on Seldom Seen Slim, as seen here. He was the featured guest of the celebration. (Murray.)

The funeral for Seldom Seen Slim, the last of Ballarat's old-timers, was held on August 17, 1968. The pallbearers are, from left to right, (foreground) Ted Lang, George Boon, and Norman A. Riggle; (background) Tom G. Murray, Cy Babcock, and George Clark. (Murray.)

On March 15, 1969, a plaque was dedicated to Seldom Seen Slim. The women in this photograph are from the Trona VFW post. They served as the color guards. At the ceremony, George Pipkin shared with the attendees some of the stories (and tall tales) about Slim and Ballarat.

Two

DARWIN

Located only a few miles from the current Death Valley National Park boundary, the mining town of Darwin boomed in 1874 and was bust by 1879. One of the popular and often repeated stories about Darwin is that "out of 124 in Darwin's "Boot Hill" graveyard, only 2 died a natural death." Although an exaggeration, the number of confirmed instances of violence, gunfights, and homicides in Darwin made it one of the most violent towns in the American West in the last quarter of the 19th century.

The discovery of the Darwin area's first mine is credited to the Brown brothers in November 1874, even though the actual discovery was made in October 1874 by a Mexican named Raphael Cuervo. By the time the New Coso Mining District was created in December 1874, Cuervo's claim had been "relocated," which is a nice, legal way of saying "jumped." Through the dubious efforts of the district's recorder, Abner Elder (former sheriff of Inyo County and associate of Pat Reddy), Cuervo's original location was disallowed. The claim subsequently passed into the hands of Reddy, who successfully defended its title in all subsequent court proceedings. In fact, this was a fairly common practice in the area. Most, if not all, of the Mexicans lost their claims or sold out for a fraction of their worth.

By 1876, Darwin had six furnaces and a population approaching 4,000. The Defiance group of mines in Darwin produced 1.5 million ounces of silver from 1874 to 1883, and the New Coso group produced 250,000 ounces of silver and 2 million pounds of lead through April 1, 1877.

When the boom ended, many Darwin residents followed its newspaper to Bodie, while others, including gunmen and lawyers, went to Tombstone and figured prominently in the gunfight at the OK Corral in the Arizona Territory on October 25, 1881.

Perhaps Oliver Roberts, known as the "Bad Man from Bodie," summed it up best when he said, "At one time there were more bad men and desperadoes in that town [Darwin] than in any of its size in the world."

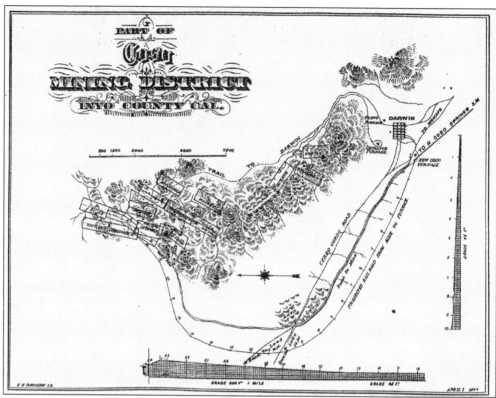

This mining map of the New Coso District shows the location of the town of Darwin (upper right) and its surrounding major mining features. At this time, the townsite comprised one square mile, and the population of Darwin and the outlying areas was over 4,000 inhabitants.

This is the earliest known photograph of Darwin, taken in 1886. The photograph was taken after the boom ended, but the town was not completely abandoned. A two-story building is visible, still standing at the end of Main Street. At this time, Darwin still had a population of about 85.

Darwin's jail still stands in the wash on the edge of town. Although Darwin was one of the most violent towns in the entire American West, its jail did not house any of its criminal lawbreakers. Though sorely needed, it was not built until just after the town's decline.

A weathered wooden grave marker, with the barely visible initials "J.T.L.," stands in the Darwin cemetery. This marker indicates the last resting place of John "Jack" T. Lloyd, who was shot and killed when the Wells Fargo stage to Darwin was held up on February 14, 1877. The highwaymen were after money intended for disbursement in Darwin. In the act of trying to shoot Wells Fargo detective Rob Paul, the robbers accidently hit passenger Lloyd.

John Wilson located the Defiance mine on December 16, 1874. The Defiance was Darwin's largest-producing mine, and its most profitable. Wilson partnered with Ned Reddy in Darwin's Capitol Saloon. This stock certificate is made out to John Wilson for 7,300 shares in the Defiance Mining Company, which was controlled by Pat Reddy, Ned Reddy, and John Wilson.

The "Old Darwin School House" (pictured) was also known as "The Black House" and the "Black School House." Built in 1876–1877, it originally served as a restaurant, then a saloon. It became the school building and operated as such from 1899 to 1917.

For many years, J.J. "Jack" Gunn was a Death Valley area resident. He was the longest-living inhabitant of the eastern Death Valley region. As early as 1875, the Inyo County Great Register lists him as living in Darwin. He operated the Minnietta mine in Lookout from 1883 until 1918. In Darwin, Gunn owned and operated the Black Metal Saloon, also known as Gunn's Saloon. (ECM.)

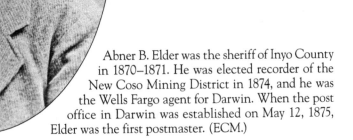

Abner B. Elder was the sheriff of Inyo County in 1870–1871. He was elected recorder of the New Coso Mining District in 1874, and he was the Wells Fargo agent for Darwin. When the post office in Darwin was established on May 12, 1875, Elder was the first postmaster. (ECM.)

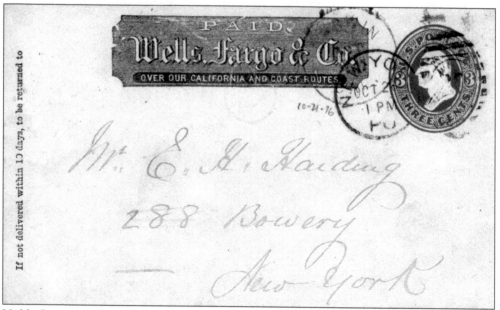

Unlike Panamint, Darwin did have a Wells Fargo express office. This cover was sent from Darwin in October 1876, when Charles Sharp was the Wells Fargo agent. The accompanying letter was written by R.C. Jacobs, one of the founders of Panamint. The letter discusses the Modoc and Minnietta mines, as well as prospects in Darwin and Panamint.

This is the Lucky Jim mine in Darwin, which Comstock mogul and US senator George Hearst bought for $50,000 in May 1875. Hearst then formed the New Coso Mining Company. The Lucky Jim, along with the Christmas Gift mine, was developed rapidly. By 1877, the production from both mines amounted to approximately 227,000 ounces of silver and 1,900,000 pounds of lead.

The caption on this photograph reads: "Office and boarding house at Lucky Jim. There are about 100 burros around here. They hang around the cook house like dogs begging for scraps. Darwin, California." After decades of little production, in 1907, the Lucky Jim mine was shipping lead-silver ore to Salt Lake smelters. A total of 40,400 tons was mined up to 1924.

It was inevitable that a few of the hundreds of burros that lived nearby wandered inside the works at the Lucky Jim mine in Darwin. In 1919, the Lucky Jim and Christmas Gift mines were still going strong, due to an increase in the price of silver. Lucky Jim was placed on the New York Stock Exchange in 1920. In 1928, the Lucky Jim mine was destroyed by fire.

The most prominent marker in the Darwin cemetery is a tall white marble obelisk marking the grave of Nancy Williams. A popular madam, she was murdered on September 12, 1877, by robbers who beat her head in with a blunt instrument. Although a large reward was offered, the killers were never caught.

This photograph seems to show Darwin as primarily a town of tents. In reality, the photograph shows a new "Tent City" in the 1910s, as mining made a comeback and brought Darwin back to life. This later tent city was located on Darwin Development Company property, about a mile before reaching the site of Darwin's Main Street.

Domingo Etcharren codiscovered the Keane Wonder mine in Death Valley. He used his share of the profits to add to his Darwin land holdings, purchasing the general store as well as the hotel and related buildings from Darwin pioneer Charles Anthony. Silas Reynolds was the "& Co." and co-owner.

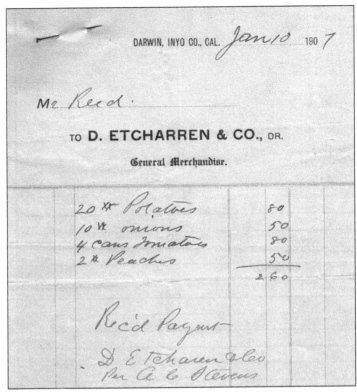

DARWIN, INYO CO., CAL. Jan 10 190 7

Mr Reed:

TO **D. ETCHARREN & CO.,** DR.

General Merchandise.

20 ℔ Potatoes	80
10 ℔ onions	50
4 cans Tomatoes	80
2 ℔ Peaches	50
	2 60

Rec'd Payment

D E Tcharren & Co

Per A C Stevens

Men walk to the Black Metal Saloon along Main Street in Darwin in 1915. The Black Metal Saloon was the prominent saloon in Darwin during the first decades of the 20th century. This photograph was taken by Mamie Reynolds, Inyo County recorder and wife of Darwin merchant Silas Reynolds.

The caption on this photograph reads "Darwin—Frank Butler property." Frank Butler was the stepson of Jim Butler, the discoverer of Tonopah, Nevada. The town was originally named Butler. Canvas tent buildings have been set up; one of them boasts a sign proclaiming it a "Saloon." One of the ubiquitous Darwin burros is visible on the far left.

Frank Butler is identified as the owner of this Darwin property as well. He formed the Summers and Butler Cattle Company with John and Charlie Summers. During the winter, they ran their cattle in Darwin and Coso. In February 1928, Frank Butler was arrested with five others in connection with the June 5, 1927, dynamiting of Los Angeles Water and Power's Cottonwood Power House in Owens Valley.

Posing for a photograph on Darwin's Main Street are, from left to right, Jeannie Carthery (O'Malley), Christina Silva (Heitman), Mattie Jane Long (Etcharren), Catalina Loughrey (Kennedy), Josephine Loughrey, Maybelle Loughrey, Ada Loughrey, an unidentified baby, and Mrs. Sweet, who was the sister of Mrs. Harry Floyd (Lucille). The Longs' house is on the right, and Jack Gunn's house is on the left.

The main intersection in Darwin is the corner of Main and Market Streets. Shown here are the remains of the visible loader gas pumps from the long-dormant Shell gas station. At far right is The Outpost, which served as a restaurant, a post office, and an office for the tourist cabins in the late 1920s and the 1930s. The old Miner's Union Hall is visible across the street.

BRIEF HISTORY OF DARWIN

Darwin, elevation 4750 ft., with 48 Whites, 19 Indians, 500 burros, was founded in 1874. 4,500 population in 1877, the same as Los Angeles at the time. Patrick Ready laid our pipeline in 1875 when there were 20 saloons on Main St. Mr. Colt settled all disputes. Boot Hill is one mile west. Fire has destroyed Darwin 3 times. But one original building remains. At Fort Coso, 7 miles west, Indians, on 3 occasions, massacred Whites. Two miles farther is Old Coso gold camp, flourishing in the late 50's. Three miles away is Cole Springs, where Mexicans recovered millions in gold, using arrastas. Thirteen miles from Cole Springs is King's Canyon, site of prehistoric petroglyphs. Vasques, noted bandit, traveled this same road. Darwin's jail has never housed a prisoner. There is no judge, sheriff nor bootleggers. This is a lead-silver district, Mexicans discovering first ore in the late '40's.

Three-fingered Jack, noted early day California bandit, was killed in Darwin, which is the gateway to Death Valley via Townsend Pass route to Stove Pipe Wells.

A business card from The Outpost Cabin Hotel in Darwin notes that it is the "outpost on your way to Death Valley." Darwin was the western gateway to Death Valley until 1934, when Highway 190 opened and bypassed the town. The unoccupied cabins as well as the visible loader gas pumps from the Shell gas station can be seen at the corner of Market and Main Streets today.

The reverse side of The Outpost business card gives a brief (and somewhat inaccurate) history of the town. As in many other Western towns trying to survive a boom, an "enhanced history" was used by businesses to try to make Darwin a tourist destination after the mines closed.

Tourist cabins were constructed behind The Outpost to take advantage of the tourism boom to Death Valley created by the Eichbaum toll road, which started just outside of Darwin and ran to Bungalette City. This road effectively made Darwin the western gateway to Death Valley until State 190 was built, bypassing Darwin.

The famous Darwin dugout dweller "Copperstain Bill" Finnimore was the cook for the Eichbaum toll road construction crew. He lived in this dugout in the Lucky Jim Wash during the Depression.

Unlike many Death Valley boomtowns, Darwin did not die. Sporadic mining kept Darwin alive until 1926, when the Eichbaum toll road was built from Darwin to Death Valley. At this time, Darwin began accommodating tourists. Highway 190 opened in 1934 and bypassed Darwin. During World War II, however, Darwin became a major lead producer. It barely clings to life today, with about 35 residents and a post office, but no other services whatsoever.

Theodore Peterson is dressed up for his portrait photograph, taken in 1907. In the 1910s, he served as justice of the peace for Darwin. In 1917, Peterson built a new hotel on Main Street, which promptly burned down on August 17, 1917, in Darwin's second major fire. He subsequently built and opened a garage, which served the tourist traffic into Death Valley.

This photograph of Darwin's downtown was taken just before it received new life during the first decade of the 20th century. Shown are the buildings that survived the great 1879 fire. Unfortunately, a fire in 1917 burned many of the buildings on the east side of Main Street, and in 1918, a blaze destroyed many buildings on the west side of Main Street.

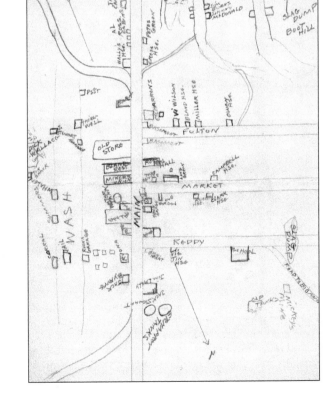

A hand-drawn map of Darwin in the 1920s shows what was left of the town at the time it was struggling to survive. The Eichbaum toll road to Stovepipe Wells had not been built, and Darwin had not seen the short-lived tourist boom that the road would provide. The Outpost tourist cabins also had not yet been built; their location was occupied by the Ross Pool Hall and the Square Deal restaurant.

Jack Gunn's Black Metal Saloon is shown here on the right. Farther down the street is Theodore Peterson's tent. Alex Rouna (left), Wallace Campbell (center), and Jimmie Carthery sit on the steps of Charles Anthony's original hotel. The two blocks on the right burned down in the August 17, 1917, fire. The two blocks on the left burned down on July 7, 1918.

Darwin was named after Dr. Erasmus Darwin French, who prospected in the area in 1850 and 1860, searching for the lost Gunsight lode. Very few of the original buildings of the 1875–1879 period remain in Darwin today. The town suffered three catastrophic fires, as well as numerous smaller ones. The wood frame buildings were not designed to withstand the harsh desert and the press of time.

A little girl identified as "Max" plays with her dog in the middle of Main Street in Darwin. The building at left is the Miner's Union Hall. On the right is the Miners Claim Café (identified as the Blaine Restaurant in the map on page 43).

The town shown here has been variously described as Darwin and as Lookout. It is actually a view of Darwin's Main Street in 1916. Just visible on the far left is the original hotel. A little dog stands on the wooden sidewalk in front of the post office, and a burro is in front of Loughrey's restaurant. These buildings burned down in the 1918 fire. (ECM.)

Beginning in 1919, Darwin's largest mines consolidated into one company, and construction began on a large-scale development of a company town. The buildings shown here were erected at this time. Abandoned remnants of the company town can still be seen today on the left side of the road coming into town.

In the early 1970s, the isolation and solitude of the ghostly setting of Darwin provided an ideal venue for sculptor Gordon Newell. Prior to coming to Darwin, Newell taught at Chouinard Art School. He was married to Academy Award nominee Gloria Stuart and created the Haupt Fountains in Washington, DC. Newell (center) is seen here in his Darwin studio with Bobby Palazzo (right) and Robert Varlotta.

Three

LOOKOUT, COSO, AND POINTS WEST

Many people are confused when they come upon the geographic name "Coso," and rightfully so. Coso can refer to the town of Old Coso, the town of Coso Hot Springs, the Coso Mountain Range, the Coso Mining District, Coso Old Fort or Fort Coso, and the New Coso Mining District (originally a part of the Coso Mining District). The Coso Mining District was established in 1860 after the discovery of silver ore by the exploration party led by Erasmus Darwin French, who was looking for the lost Gunsight mine. At the center of the district, the town of Coso was established. In the mid-1870s, new discoveries led to the formation of the New Coso Mining District and the town of Darwin. At this time, the name of the town of Coso became Old Coso. Much of the Coso Mining District adjoins and is located within the current Death Valley National Park boundary.

Approximately 10 miles southwest of Old Coso lay the ruins of Coso Hot Springs. Native Americans of the region used the springs for cultural and healing rituals. In the 1920s, it became a popular vacation spot, advertised as the "Greatest Natural Radiant Hot Spring in America." Coso Hot Springs was abandoned in 1944, when the US Navy took over the property and created the China Lake Naval Weapons Center.

The town of Lookout, formed in May 1875, consisted of several stores, a number of buildings constructed of rock and wood, and, of course, numerous saloons. The Lookout District, located about 12 miles east of Darwin, was also known as the Modoc District. Lookout was not as violent as Darwin, its nearest neighbor, and Panamint, but it did have its share of gunfights.

Transportation for the area on the east side of Death Valley was centered in Keeler, which was the terminus of the Carson & Colorado Railroad. Keeler also ran stages to Darwin and Panamint, with stops in between.

Originally known as Granite Springs, the town of Coso is located in the Coso Mountain Range, about four miles east-southeast of Coso Peak. Almost all of the buildings in the town of Coso were made of stone, so, although the town has been completely abandoned for well over a century, foundations still remain.

In 1860, when the discovery of rich ore was made by Dr. Darwin French and his party, the Coso Mining District was formed. Many prospectors flooded the area, establishing the town of Coso. The Mining Laws for the Coso Mining District (shown here) were written entirely in Spanish, and the area became generally known as "The Spanish Mines." Coso had a population of about 300 by July 1860.

At the end of the 1870s, Coso was becoming a ghost town. Although a few prospectors remained, the site was soon abandoned completely. An occasional prospector would repurpose a building and make it home for a while. Now, the ruins of the town of Old Coso are entirely located within the restricted boundaries of the China Lake Naval Weapons Center. (George Koenig.)

Coso Old Fort, also known as Fort Coso, was located in Coso Canyon at Darwin Springs, about eight miles from Darwin. It was built in the 1860s as an outpost of Camp Independence during the period of fierce battles between local Indians and settlers. Shown here are the remains of the barracks building, including a fireplace, at Fort Coso.

The short-lived town of Lookout was formed in 1875. It boomed in 1877 and declined rapidly after that. This photograph of Lookout at its peak shows Main Street looking to the west, with the Argus Range in the background. The house in the center of the photograph was the residence of constable Frank Fitzgerald and his wife, Marie. (ECM.)

Frank Fitzgerald was affectionately known as "Little Fitz." While a constable at Lookout, he was involved in a gunfight in which he shot and killed Augustine Moran. In another fight, with Oliver Roberts, Fitzgerald shot two men named Dickey and Shay. Fitzgerald also served as constable in Darwin and as postmaster of Modock. (ECM.)

This view looks west toward Lookout Mountain. Handwritten at the top are the relative locations of the Minnietta mine (barely visible on the far left), Lookout Mountain, the "Upper Town" of Lookout, the "Lower Town" of Lookout, and the road leading to Lookout and to the Modoc mine.

The only remnant of the large milling operation in Lookout is this boiler. The name of its manufacturer, "CMC Corp," is embossed on its side. A narrow footpath is just visible in the center of the photograph, which was taken from the east in the 1950s.

Before Oliver Roberts became known as the "Bad Man from Bodie," he built his reputation in the Lookout District. In Lookout, Roberts shot Jack McGinnis. He also teamed up with Frank Fitzgerald in a gunfight against Dickey and Shay. Roberts and Fitzgerald partnered again during Darwin's War in 1878, when Constable Fitzgerald deputized Roberts.

Shown here is the most prominent ruin in Lookout's "lower town." This building was originally the main store in Lookout during its boom period. These remains are of the basement or lower floor. The photograph was taken in the late 1950s or early 1960s.

The Modoc District was established on the east slope of the Argus Range, 15 miles southeast of Darwin. Producing mines were the Minnietta and Modoc. In 1876, the Modoc and the Lookout smelters were bought by George C. Hearst, who formed the Modock Consolidated Mines Co. Shown here is the road into Modoc from Stone Canyon. (George Koenig.)

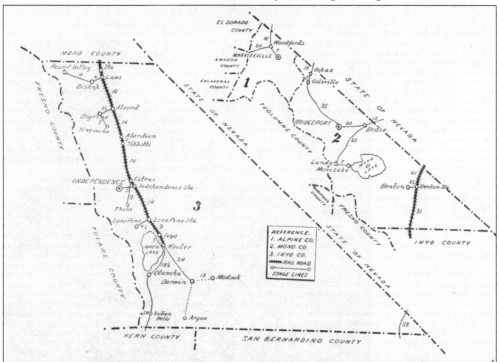

This 1897 map shows the towns, county roads, and stage lines carrying passengers, mail, and express. In the Death Valley region, only Darwin and Modock are listed, as the first boom period of the 1870s had faded. The next boom would not start until a few years later, at the beginning of the 20th century.

The Modoc mine hired John Kelly to do its assessment work for 1915. Here, Kelly and his burros prepare to leave Darwin for Modock. Many of Darwin's 25 residents were on hand for the send-off. Henry Heitman is sitting on the burro, and Kelly is standing to the right behind him. George, an Indian, is on the porch. Silas Reynolds is at far left, and Mrs. Etcharren and her small son Ted are left of center.

In 1876, the Minnietta Belle Silver Mining Company was formed. The Minnietta mine had a rather low production until 1895, when Frank Fitzgerald worked the mine and recovered $65,000 in silver and $600 in gold. Jack Gunn worked the mine for a time in the 1890s. (George Koenig.)

During Jack Gunn's operation, the Minnietta mine had produced over $350,000 in silver and $25,000 in gold. The mine and buildings surrounding it were abandoned from 1920 to 1944, when mining production became profitable due to the demand created by World War II. The estimated production for the Minnietta mine from 1895 to 1955 is $600,000.

The short-lived mining town of Reilly was named for Edward Reilly, who purchased mining claims in the area. By January 1883, Reilly had a store, hotel, barns, corrals, and a blacksmith shop. The United States established a post office in Reilly on January 22, 1883, with R.C. Spear as postmaster. Reilly's 10-stamp mill made its first run just as the post office was closing in October 1883.

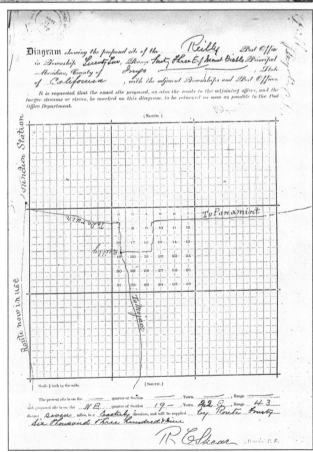

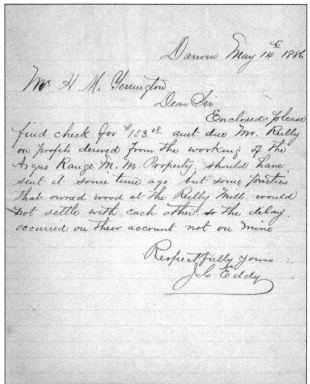

This 1886 letter refers to Edward Reilly and his Argus Range mining properties. Reilly was located about 30 miles southeast of Darwin, on the western edge of Panamint Valley. In 1882, Edward Reilly formed the Argus Range Silver Mining Company with a capitalization of $200,000. By the end of 1883, the town disappeared. On modern maps, its site is referred to as "Anthony Mill Ruins," despite the fact that Charles Anthony probably did not have much, if anything, to do with them.

The western towns of Death Valley were served by the Carson & Colorado Railroad at Keeler, then by stages or wagons that would carry passengers and supplies to Darwin, Panamint, and other locales. This 1907 photograph shows the Keeler stage heading to Mojave. The 125-mile trip took three days down and three days back, with one day to rest. (NPS.)

The town of Keeler was named for Julius M. Keeler. He founded Pacific University in Oregon, then served as a captain in the 5th Connecticut Infantry during the Civil War. He is shown here with his wife. After the war, Keeler moved to Inyo, engaged in mining enterprises, and prepared the first comprehensive mining map of Inyo County.

The hot springs at Coso were a destination for Native American tribes for centuries. They bathed in the springs for medicinal purposes and celebrated religious ceremonies there as well. This photograph was taken at the spring before the town and resort of Coso Hot Springs were built.

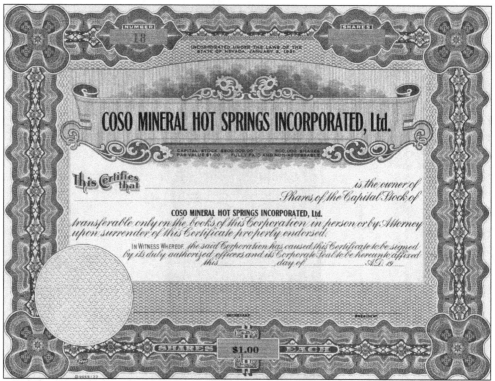

In 1918, F.J. Sanders formed a company to construct buildings at Coso Hot Springs for guest accommodations and for mud and thermal baths. Sanders operated the resort town from 1920 until 1927, when he lost the property in foreclosure. A new company, Coso Mineral Hot Springs Incorporated, Ltd., was formed on January 3, 1931, to operate the resort and to bottle and sell the medicinal mineral water.

In 1944, when the Navy took over all of the land in the surrounding area for its weapons testing, access to the entire town was restricted, and tourists were no longer accommodated. As a result of the restricted access, the remains of the town have not been extensively vandalized, as seen in this 1960s official US Navy photograph.

The remains of a visible loader gasoline pump from the Coso Hot Springs service station are shown here. The empty rectangular frame on the right of the tank would have held a cardboard sign with the price, which would have been about 19¢ per gallon at the time the station was in operation.

The town of Millspaugh was located east of the Argus summit, at the head of Shepherd Canyon. It was on the toll road that ran from Lone Pine through Darwin, then to Old Coso, across Etcharren Valley into Panamint Valley, and ended at Panamint City. In this photograph, the post office and store building is in the center, tent buildings are on the right, and the mill is on the left.

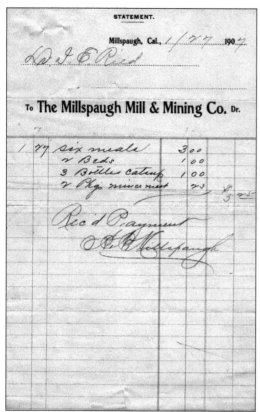

While prospecting with two friends, Almon N. Millspaugh located producing ore while on his way to Ballarat. Unlike most Death Valley mining towns, the town of Millspaugh was owned by family members and not by outside investors. The Millspaugh store was located in the same building as the post office.

The Millspaugh Post Office was located in the building at center. The post office sign can be seen above the porch. The Millspaugh Post Office was established on March 15, 1902, and it operated until July 30, 1910. Almon N. Millspaugh, the man standing on the porch, was its only postmaster.

Four

GREENWATER

The great gold discoveries in Bullfrog and Rhyolite drew thousands of prospectors and miners to the Death Valley area, and they staked claims for many miles. Newcomers had to expand their search for riches; ultimately, that search led to the Greenwater Valley. Just who made the actual discovery that led to the mining boom in Greenwater is a bit murky. Shorty Harris claimed to have made the original discovery, but said his partner failed to record the claims. Arthur Kunze is credited with being "the Father of Greenwater," but it was John Salsberry who backed Kunze in forming the Greenwater Copper Company and staked some of the first prospects. Ultimately, Fred Birney and Phil Creasor, who found a rich copper ledge while looking for gold, recorded their claims. Their samples assayed so high that Montana copper magnate Patsy Clark bought Birney and Creasor's claims, incorporated the Furnace Creek Copper Company, and sold shares in New York, San Francisco, and elsewhere. The rush was on.

While it was copper and not gold that fueled Greenwater's boom, it had all the excitement of a typical gold rush. Unfortunately, two events led to Greenwater's spectacular fall: the economic panic of 1907, which dried up capital and sank the country into a depression; and the fact that a combined total of only about $2,600 worth of copper was ever sold from the over 73 incorporated mining companies, which had a total capitalization of almost a quarter of a billion dollars.

It has been reported that Greenwater had the shortest life ever recorded for a boom camp of its size, estimated at over 2,000 people at its peak. Greenwater began as a desolate expanse of inhospitable desert and grew into a district with four towns (Greenwater, Ramsey, Kunze, and Furnace), hotels, newspapers, saloons, freighting companies, brokerage houses, markets, and more. In less than four years, it was down to a population of zero. "Dad" Fairbanks ran the last store and saloon in Greenwater. When he left for Shoshone, he took all the remaining buildings with him.

Women were scarce in mining camps in the West, especially in the Death Valley area. This couple poses for a portrait outside of their one-room tent house in Greenwater in 1907. The shadows of both the photographer and his camera are visible in the lower left.

TONOPAH LUMBER CO.

GREENWATER YARD

JOHN J. KAVANAGH, MANAGER

LUMBER AND ALL KINDS OF BUILDING MATERIAL

GREENWATER, CALIF.,

March 27/07

Mr Jno Salsberry

Tonopah Nevada.

Dear Sir. When Mr. Merry left here with you he said he was going to write me and place some money in the Bank for me to check against. I have paid one small bill and I have a lumber bill of about 400.00 against the Co. Cent, M. Co. There will be other bills which should be met as they are presented and besides the labor on the shaft I presume will have to be paid every month. I wish you would put the matter before Mr Merry and have him attend to the matter at once.

Have you seen my claims at Mina, and what do you think of them.

Respectfully,

John J. Kavanagh.

The Tonopah Lumber Co., controlled by John Salsberry, supplied almost all of the lumber and building materials for construction of the more substantial buildings in Greenwater. The company brought in so much that it established an office and lumberyard in the town of Greenwater itself in order to facilitate distribution.

This early automobile, a model 1906 Stearns, is stopped on the Greenwater toll road, about halfway between Rhyolite and Greenwater. Although it was a five-passenger vehicle, the seats are piled high with mining equipment and provisions. The driver may have been a mining promoter, since this car cost over $4,000 when new. The photograph was taken in 1907.

Dogs were pressed into service by the Brin & Bernstein store, which sold general merchandise and mine supplies in Greenwater. The dog on the left is identified as "Brin," and the dog on the right as "Bernstein." Both dogs are towing carts made out of boxes. Brin's cart is made out of a Tanglefoot flypaper box. A Cream of Wheat box lays on its side next to the wood cabin, perhaps to be used for another cart.

The caption on this photograph reads "Brin & Bernstein's Messenger Service, Greenwater, Calif." The messenger service consisted of dogs that were trained to deliver packages to houses and businesses in Greenwater. R.M. Brin and Sol Bernstein were successful merchants in Oregon and Beatty, Nevada, before opening their store in Greenwater.

While Death Valley is known for its 20-mule teams, the caption of this photograph reads "Eighteen Horse Team Hauling Lumber to Greenwater." By September 1906, the Tonopah Lumber Co. reported that it had sold 150,000 board feet of lumber in Greenwater. The demand for lumber continued until the boom ended. Rhyolite photographer A.E. Holt captured this view in April 1907.

On the back of this photograph, Donald B. Gillies described his trip to the Greenwater area. "On the way to Death Valley. Water barrels, (2) added later at the last water hole. Parked at Furnace Creek and remained there for 36 hours 'Scouting Around'. Route was along the foothills 'Furnace Range' Mountains." Gillies represented Charles Schwab's interests in the Bullfrog District, and Schwab purchased the Montgomery Shoshone mine on the basis of Gillies's recommendation.

The caption attached to this photograph reads: "Two mining moguls with their driver on their way into the Death Valley area to inspect the latest find at the copper camp of Greenwater. This Tourist automobile was manufactured in Los Angeles for a few years. It was a very successful vehicle for traveling the desert sands."

As can be seen in this photograph, the weather can be extreme in Death Valley. Although the region has the hottest recorded temperature on Earth, this image records the streets and buildings of Greenwater covered in snow on November 9, 1906, after a freak snowstorm dropped over a foot of snow.

Carl Glasscock (right) talks with Indian George Hansen. Carl Burgess Glasscock, along with Curt E. Kunze, established Greenwater's newspaper, the *Death Valley Chuck-Walla*, after arriving in Greenwater with just one year's experience with the *San Francisco Examiner*. Kunze's brother Arthur put up the money, and Glasscock's brother did the printing.

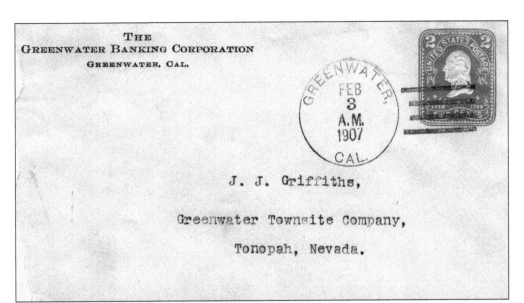

This envelope was mailed from the Greenwater Banking Corporation to J.J. Griffiths of the Greenwater Townsite Company. It was postmarked at the Greenwater Post Office on February 3, 1907. In 1909, the building used by the short-lived Greenwater Banking Corporation was moved by Ralph J. "Dad" Fairbanks to Shoshone, where it still stands today.

The town of Kunze is shown in this 1906 photograph. Kunze was located about two miles west of the current location of Greenwater and, confusingly, was also known as Greenwater. Kunze was named after Greenwater's founder, prospector Arthur Kunze, who discovered the first copper claims in the area and who served as Greenwater's first postmaster.

The town of Ramsey is seen here in 1906. Adding to the confusion of the Kunze/Greenwater original townsite, Harry Ramsey started a town that he called, variously, Ramsey, Copperfield, and Greenwater. In November 1906, John Salsberry acquired control of the Ramsey townsite. Salsberry reestablished the town of Greenwater in an improved location. In order to entice residents of Kunze to move, Salsberry featured new lots and offered to pay all moving costs.

"Alkali Bill" Brong is shown driving *The Desert Flyer* on its way through Death Valley from Rhyolite, Nevada, and heading to Greenwater. *The Desert Flyer* was an auto stage, considered to be the "modern way of travelling between mining camps in Nevada."

Although the Greenwater boom was largely based on a financial mining scam, many of the locals honestly believed in the town and its success. This is evident from the $5,000 stock certificate shown here, issued to Greenwater store owner R.M. Brin. The certificate is signed by company president Arthur Kunze, the founder of Greenwater. He was also its first postmaster and the eponym of Kunze, the original name of the town.

Charles M. Schwab, the president of Carnegie Steel, was a major investor in Rhyolite and the largest promoter of the copper mines in Greenwater. Here, Schwab and his party are seen in front of the Southern Hotel in Rhyolite, about to leave for Greenwater to survey their holdings.

Mining promoters would charter automobiles to take prospective investors from Rhyolite (which was served by three different railroads) to Greenwater. There, they would be shown various mining prospects and plied with drinks and food to encourage them to take advantage of a "can't miss" investment opportunity.

Goldfield, Nevada, *July 21* 1906

M *Jno Salisbury*

To **Nevada Mobile Transit Company,** Dr.

July 16	To 2 days Trip to Greenwater Spgs Xrot.	450. —
21	" 4 Siemens tubes	72. —
	" toll over Company's road (6 down 3 ret.)	75.
	Less	597.
Received Payment.		5
Nevada Mob. T. Co.		592.00

John Salsberry, known as "the Nevada Copper King," owned substantial interests in Greenwater, including the Greenwater Copper Company, which he organized with Arthur Kunze, and the Tonopah Lumber Company, which supplied all of Greenwater's wood. In July 1906, he hired a car for a three-day trip to Greenwater, which cost him almost $600, including $72 for four inner tubes and $75 for tolls over the roads.

Despite the town's name, water had to be brought to Greenwater, as it was not available in any of its competing townsites. When John Salsberry acquired the Ramsey site, he hired 18-horse teams to haul water to it in order to encourage the residents of Kunze to relocate. Salsberry sold the water for $7.50 per barrel, but he claimed he lost $600 a month doing so.

While Greenwater did not have a Wells Fargo office, this receipt indicates that John Salsberry utilized the services of Wells Fargo in Tonopah to ship goods to his partner J.V. Stewart in Greenwater in December 1906. Coincidentally, the January 15, 1907, issue of the *Death Valley Chuck-Walla* mentioned a Wells Fargo strongbox found near Willow Springs in the Funeral Range.

FUNERAL RANGE COPPER COMPANY

GENERAL OFFICE
TONOPAH, NEVADA

MINES AT
COPPERFIELD, INYO CO., CAL.

Copperfield, Inyo Co., Cal., *Aug 29* 190*6*

To _Henry Butcher_ _____ Dr.

for labor _____ | 3 | 00

Approved for Payment:

_____
Superintendent

Aug 29 190*6*

Received of FUNERAL RANGE COPPER COMPANY

Three & 00/100

Dollars,

Please date and sign this voucher and
return to Funeral Range Copper Company,
Tonopah, Nev.

in full of above account.

$ *3.00*

W H Butcher

This Funeral Range Copper Company invoice of August 29, 1906, is from Copperfield. Harry Ramsey insisted on calling his townsite Greenwater, although it was commonly called Ramsey and, less commonly, Copperfield. Whatever it was called, its location was hard to determine. It was variously described as being one to four miles east or southeast of Kunze's camp. Harry Ramsey also moved his site around at least once. He vigorously promoted his own town.

Ralph J. "Dad" Fairbanks (at center in white hat) stands next to his wife, Celeste, at their home in Shoshone. Dad Fairbanks ran the last store and saloon in Greenwater, the Furnace Mercantile. In 1910, he left Greenwater and took its remaining buildings to found the town of Shoshone.

This first issue of Greenwater's newspaper, the *Death Valley Chuck-Walla*, was printed on butcher paper. The paper's mission statement, printed on the first page, reads: "Published on the desert at the brink of Death Valley. Mixing the dope, cool from the mountains and hot from the desert, and withal putting out a concoction with which you can do as you damn please as soon as you have paid for it. Price, Ten Cents."

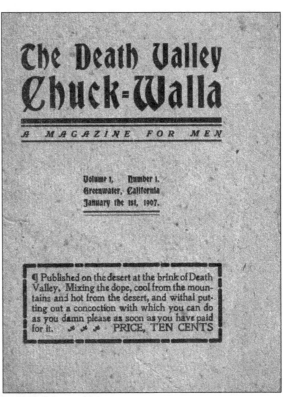

Jolise Samson (or Dawson) is shown in front of his tent cabin at Ramsey in July 1906. At the time this photograph was taken, Harry Ramsey had organized the Greenwater Townsite Company, and the town of Ramsey had a population of 200, with a restaurant, two saloons, a hotel, and a store.

On the back of this photograph is written, "Where was Greenwater? A long line of tents . . . an occasional wooden building and the burro on the path—Greenwater nestled against the Funeral Mountains of Death Valley in June 1907."

The employees of Greenwater's newspaper, the *Death Valley Chuck-Walla*, pose for a photograph outside their office. The first issue, in January 1907, contained the article "A Town on Wheels," which described Greenwater: "pandemonium reigns. Saloons and boarding houses, stores, and brokerage firms are doing business on the run and trying to be on both sides of the mountain at one time."

Curt E. Kunze (left) and Carl B. Glasscock, publishers and editors of the *Death Valley Chuck-Walla*, are shown in front of the newspaper's office. The photograph was taken by A.E. Holt in April 1907. A fire on June 22, 1907, destroyed the *Chuck-Walla* offices as well as those of its competitor, the *Greenwater Times*, which had been recently bought out by Kunze and Glasscock.

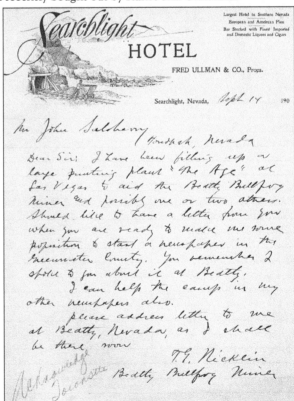

On September 14, 1906, newspaper magnate T.G. Nicklin asked John Salsberry to make him a proposition to start a newspaper in the Greenwater Country, noting, "I can help the camp in my other newspapers also." With his brother, Nicklin owned and ran other newspapers in the Death Valley area, including the *Bullfrog Miner*, the *Beatty Bullfrog Miner*, and the *Las Vegas Age*.

Miners of the Greenwater Saratoga Copper Company pose for a photograph in front of the mine's hoist. The company was incorporated in 1906, but, as was the case with almost all of the other mines, by 1908, it sat idle. There were plans to sink a crosscut in 1909, but they never materialized, and the town died.

Hopes for Greenwater were still high when Borax Smith incorporated the Tonopah & Greenwater Railroad in March 1907. The Tonopah & Greenwater was only one of three proposed railroads to survey running track to the copper boomtown of Greenwater. Unfortunately, by the time the proposed railroad could get financing and engineering in place, the boom was over, and the road was never built.

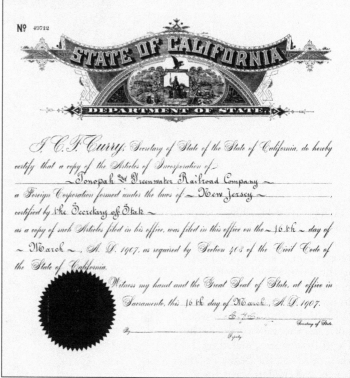

In November 1906, one of the water wagons serving the holding tanks of the town broke down. In the ensuing panic, water prices went to $20 per barrel before the wagon could be repaired. Ingenious methods were attempted, and unusual lengths were taken, to try to solve the water problem, as illustrated in this photograph of a makeshift automobile with two large water barrels. The photograph is titled "Carry water to Greenwater."

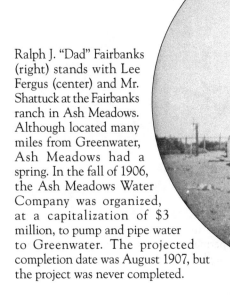

Ralph J. "Dad" Fairbanks (right) stands with Lee Fergus (center) and Mr. Shattuck at the Fairbanks ranch in Ash Meadows. Although located many miles from Greenwater, Ash Meadows had a spring. In the fall of 1906, the Ash Meadows Water Company was organized, at a capitalization of $3 million, to pump and pipe water to Greenwater. The projected completion date was August 1907, but the project was never completed.

This photograph is identified on the back as "The stage at Longstreets' ranch for Greenwater." Jack Longstreet's ranch was located in Ash Meadows. In early July 1906, the stage from Ash Meadows to Greenwater began operations. Jack Longstreet, who had been involved in a number of gunfights, was known as "the Last of the Desert Frontiersmen" and was the subject of a biography of the same name.

In 1906, when this photograph was taken, Greenwater was still in the process of being established. It was transitioning from a tent city to a town with more permanent wooden structures. There were two stores, a hotel, a restaurant, and two corrals, and an application was sent for the establishment of a post office. (Photograph by Per Larson.)

The Greenwater-Kunze Copper Company was one of John Salsberry's many Greenwater properties and investments. The company was incorporated on November 17, 1906, in order to capitalize on the speculative frenzy in Greenwater mines. Although Arthur Kunze was not an incorporator, he did retain a financial interest for use of this name. In 1907, Salsberry and his partner, J.J. Griffith, planned to build a 20-room hotel in Greenwater.

Prospectors line up for a group portrait. They are standing next to burros packed with supplies on Greenwater's main thoroughfare. Along with water, transportation remained a problem for prospectors heading to Greenwater. The auto stages were quite expensive, so many prospectors walked with their burros from Bullfrog, which took three days.

The copper frenzy of 1906 and 1907 caused a stampede to Greenwater. Mining promoters quickly staked locations and sold stock, and the town of Greenwater grew overnight. But the economic panic of 1907 and the lack of copper led to the town's demise. These three prospectors look somewhat dejected at their mine in Greenwater in February 1907. The town did not survive for much longer after this photograph was taken.

VOTE FOR . . . AND RE-ELECT

CHAS. BROWN

(INCUMBENT)

STATE SENATOR

Inyo-Mono-Alpine Counties
·
EXPERIENCE! · SENIORITY!

CONSCIENTIOUS REPRESENTATION OF THIS AREA FOR THE PAST 20 YEARS
·
Your Continued Support Respectfully Solicited

Chalfant Press

Charles Brown was the sheriff of Greenwater during its 1906–1907 boom period. He then moved to Shoshone and started a hotel with his father-in-law, Ralph J. "Dad" Fairbanks. Brown was a well-respected state senator representing the Death Valley area in Sacramento for over 24 years.

Five

Bullfrog, Rhyolite, and Points North

The huge Bullfrog-Rhyolite boom and its resulting towns can initially be traced to the Keane Wonder discovery. In 1904, Domingo Etcharren and Jack Keane discovered gold, which gave rise to a large Death Valley gold rush and led to the formation of the towns of Keane and Keane Wonder. It was this discovery that encouraged Shorty Harris and Ed Cross to prospect in that part of Death Valley.

Rhyolite, the largest town in the area, was served by three railroads: the Tonopah & Tidewater, the Las Vegas & Tonopah Railroad, and the Bullfrog Goldfield Railroad. Located only a few miles from the Inyo County line, the district had a population estimated at over 10,000 at its peak, though only ruins remain today.

At the northwestern end of Death Valley National Park lies Scotty's Castle and Ubehebe Crater. Both are popular destinations for the 21st-century visitor to Death Valley. Surprisingly, both have towns associated with them. John Salsberry and Ray T. Baker founded the Salina City townsite, which was renamed Latimer and, ultimately, Ubehebe. The townsite at its peak consisted of 20 tents, two saloons, a company store, a stage station, and a feedlot.

While most people would not consider Scotty's Castle to be a ghost town, or even a town for that matter, it did in fact have all of the attributes of a small town. It had a gas station, lodging for the public, and a post office with a government-appointed postmaster. The post office operated for a little over six years, from 1947 to 1953.

The town of Leadfield was another very short-lived town. It boomed and busted within a couple of years as a result of a stock scam based on nonexistent and/or nonproducing mines. Formed in 1925 by stock swindler C.C. Julian through his Western Lead Mine Company, Leadfield peaked in 1926 with a population of about 300. The town boasted the usual assortment of hotels, restaurants, stores, and a post office, which opened in June. By the end of 1927, the post office closed and the town was deserted.

The Keane Wonder mine and mill were located in the Bullfrog Mining District, about 22 miles south of Rhyolite. A town developed around the mining camp, and a post office operated from 1912 to 1914. The mine and the town were named for Jack Keane, who was its codiscoverer with Domingo Etcharren. (NPS.)

MEMORANDUM OF AGREEMENT.

THIS AGREEMENT, made and entered into at Tonopah, Nevada, this 4th day of December, 1905, by and between E. N. WENDKIND, of Rhyolite, Nye County, Nevada, party of the first part, and JOHN KEANE and DOMINGO ETCHERRAN, of Inyo County, State of California, party of the second part,

WITNESSETH: Whereas, negotiations have been pending between the parties hereto for the sale by the second parties and the purchase by the first party of those certain mining properties commonly known as the Keane Wonder Mines, a group of twenty claims, more or less, with appurtenant water rights, mill sites, and other valuable rights initiated and acquired upon the public domain, and ownedby the second parties, situated in South Bullfrog Mining District, Inyo County, State of California; and

Whereas, an informal agreement has beenmade and entered into whereby the second parties have given to the first party an option to purchase said properties, upon certain terms and conditions, said written agreement being preliminary to a more formal and particular agreement to be drawn hereafter as soon as the requisite data concerning said properties can be obtained from the Recorder of Inyo County, California;

Now, Therefore, in consideration of the premises, and as part of the consideration for the execution of said option, a copy of which said option agreement is hereunto attached and made a part hereof, and in consideration of other valuable considerations not herein expressed, the first party has promised, covenanted and agreed, and does hereby promise, covenant and agree to and with the second

In April 1904, Etcharren told Keane about a quartz cropping he found. Keane investigated further, found free gold, and located the claim as the Keane Wonder. This memorandum of agreement is for the sale of the Keane Wonder mine by Jack Keane and Domingo Etcharren for $500,000 in 1905.

In 1904, Shoshone Johnny was the discoverer of the largest gold mine in the Death Valley area, the Montgomery Shoshone mine in Bullfrog. Though Johnny is widely credited with the discovery, all the financial benefits went to E.A. "Bob" Montgomery, to whom Johnny showed the location. Montgomery was said to have given Johnny just a few dollars for his part in the discovery, but Montgomery always denied it.

The Montgomery Shoshone mine was named for Bob Montgomery and Shoshone Johnny. Some think that Montgomery took advantage of Johnny, but in this letter, Montgomery takes great care in explaining exactly what transpired, writing, "Johnnie did not find a claim on which good ore was ever found."

This view of Bullfrog, Nevada, at the edge of Death Valley, was taken in early December 1906. At this time, the rivalry between Rhyolite and Bullfrog for dominance over the Bullfrog District had ended with Rhyolite the victor. Bullfrog stayed alive until the collapse of the district in 1909.

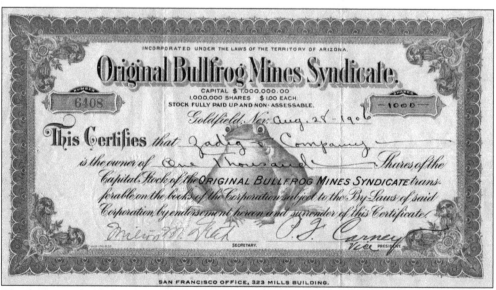

The discovery that led to the founding of the Bullfrog District was made by Shorty Harris and Ed Cross in 1904. The rush that followed brought prospectors, tents, and towns to the surrounding area. The Original Bullfrog Mines Syndicate was organized and incorporated by promoters in Goldfield to operate the original discoveries.

Ralph D. Paine wrote on the back of this 1906 photograph, "A city street in the Bullfrog District." The Bullfrog District would have included the towns of Bullfrog, Rhyolite, Gold Center, South Bullfrog, Gold Bar, and Amargosa. The towns were very close to each other, and their boundaries were not clearly defined.

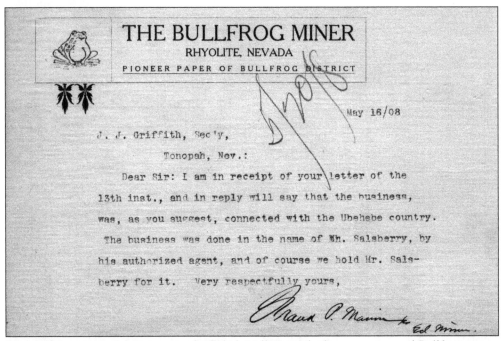

Surprisingly, many of the towns in the Death Valley area had newspapers, and Bullfrog was no different. This letter on the *Bullfrog Miner* letterhead concerns advertising that was authorized by promoter John Salsberry to generate investment in the Ubehebe mining district and to help establish other towns.

A sense of how large and important Rhyolite was is evident in this 1910 photograph. Rhyolite, the economic center of the Bullfrog Mining District, was served by three different railroads: the Tonopah & Tidewater Railroad, the Las Vegas & Tonopah Railroad, and the Bullfrog Goldfield Railroad. At its peak, Rhyolite had a population estimated at over 10,000 people, who could enjoy fine dining, luxurious hotels, and over 45 saloons.

Shown here is the Las Vegas & Tonopah Railroad station in Rhyolite. Long after the town of Rhyolite was abandoned, the station was still in use as a casino, bar, restaurant, and meeting room. Though not used commercially in many years, the building is still standing.

An elaborate Christmas dinner was staged on December 25, 1905, by the Montgomery Shoshone mine, courtesy of E.A. "Bob" Montgomery. No doubt the champagne and cigars were to celebrate his good fortune. Shortly after this sumptuous feast, Charles Schwab bought control of the company, which netted Montgomery $1 million in cash while still retaining 20-percent ownership.

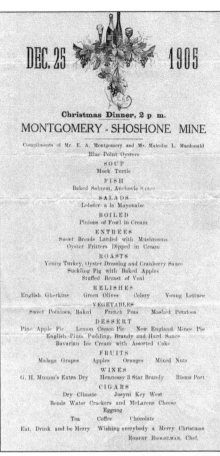

DEC. 25   1905

Christmas Dinner, 2 p. m.
MONTGOMERY - SHOSHONE MINE

Compliments of Mr. E. A. Montgomery and Mr. Malcolm L. Macdonald
Blue Point Oysters
SOUP
Mock Turtle
FISH
Baked Salmon, Anchovie Sauce
SALADS
Lobster a la Mayonaise
BOILED
Pinions of Fowl in Cream
ENTREES
Sweet Breads Larded with Mushrooms
Oyster Fritters Dipped in Cream
ROASTS
Young Turkey, Oyster Dressing and Cranberry Sauce
Suckling Pig with Baked Apples
Stuffed Breast of Veal
RELISHES
English Gherkins   Green Olives   Celery   Young Lettuce
VEGETABLES
Sweet Potatoes, Baked   French Peas   Mashed Potatos
DESSERT
Pine Apple Pie   Lemon Cream Pie   New England Mince Pie
English Plum Pudding, Brandy and Hard Sauce
Bavarian Ice Cream with Assorted Cake
FRUITS
Malaga Grapes   Apples   Oranges   Mixed Nuts
WINES
G. H. Mumm's Extra Dry   Hennessy 3 Star Brandy   Riems Port
CIGARS
Dry Climate   Josyni Key West
Bends Water Crackers and McLarens Cheese
Eggnog
Tea   Coffee   Chocolate
Eat, Drink and be Merry   Wishing everybody a Merry Christmas
ROBERT BROGELMAN, Chef.

This photograph of Rhyolite's famous Bottle House was taken in 1906, on the same day as the Rhyolite Glass House photograph on page 88. Note the more substantial building and elegant style. Tom Kelly, the builder of the house, is standing in the doorway, but he never lived in it.

The famous Bottle House was not the only such structure in Rhyolite. This "Glass House" was also made of bottles, but it is a one-room structure rather than the elaborate gingerbread-style house of the more famous version. This photograph was taken in 1906, when Rhyolite was still a combination of tents and wood frame buildings.

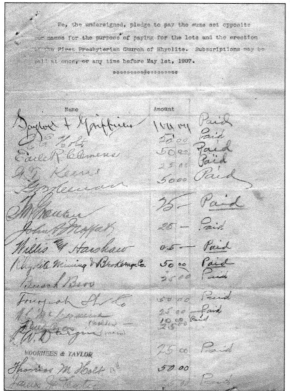

When Rev. Jay Mortimer Swander arrived in Rhyolite, there was no church and only six congregants. He took it upon himself to arrange for a subscription among the townspeople to obtain money to build a church. His efforts were successful, as seen by this eight-page subscription agreement, which contains the names and pledges of most of Rhyolite's prominent citizens.

Originally built by Rev. J.M. Swander in 1907, this building served as the First Presbyterian Church in Rhyolite. When the town of Rhyolite declined, the building was moved to Ryan, where it was put in use as the Recreation Building. This photograph was taken in Ryan and shows the building without its belfry.

While Rhyolite was reaching its peak population of almost 10,000, the beginnings of the economic downturn caused by the panic of 1907 were starting to be seen. This store on Rhyolite's Main Street has already fallen into disrepair in early 1907, with its canvas covering torn and hanging.

The most prominent ruin that remains of Rhyolite is the much-photographed John S. Cook & Company Bank building. The three-story building was erected in 1907 at a cost of $90,000. It had three-foot-thick, reinforced concrete walls, a marble stairway, stained glass, and mahogany baseboards. The Rhyolite Post Office was located in the basement.

This photograph is identified on the back as "Outside Beatty, Rube Ryan's mine and Hollywood Day Store." Located in the Bullfrog Mining District, both Rube Ryan's mine and the Hollywood Day Store were close to the Rhyolite and Bullfrog mining activities and towns.

Diamondfield, shown here in 1907, was founded in 1903 by "Diamondfield Jack" Davis, a noted gunfighter who had just been pardoned by the governor of Idaho for murder. Touted as being a rival to Goldfield, Diamonfield's fortune never materialized. By the end of 1904, Diamondfield had a post office, saloons, and other mining-camp businesses. The post office closed in 1908 and, with it, went Diamondfield.

This building was erected in 1905 as the Montgomery Hotel in Beatty, and then it was moved to Pioneer. The town of Pioneer, established in 1908, was located in the northern Bullfrog Hills. At its peak in 1908, it had a population of 2,500, a post office, lumber company, theater, hotels, saloons, restaurants, bakeries, shoe store, boardinghouses, cigar store, and a Western Union office.

This rare photograph shows a young-looking Seldom Seen Slim panning for gold in the desert. This is probably a staged photograph, since placer mining for gold was a technique rarely utilized in Death Valley, due to the scarcity of water. Slim was known to have participated in a movie shoot in the 1920s, and this could be a candid shot taken during the productions.

Schwab was a short-lived mining boomtown located in Echo Canyon. By early 1907, Schwab had a post office, telephone service, and a stage line. It was known as "A Mining Camp Built by Ladies" when three women—Mrs. F.W. Dunn, Gertrude Fessler, and Helen H. Black—took control of the town.

At the same time that the mining promotions led to the founding of Leadfield, across the border, a discovery of high-grade ore led to the development of the town of Wahmonie. The town was established in 1928 and grew to almost 1,500, then it was determined that the ore was not as good as originally thought. Like Leadfield, the town went bust. It was deserted by the end of 1928.

George Cook (left) is shown prospecting for gold in the Transvaal country, northeast of Rhyolite. The town of Transvaal was started in 1906 and contained 75 tents, 700 people, 4 saloons, an assay office, a lumberyard, a boardinghouse, 2 newspapers, and other businesses. Shortly after its founding, little valuable ore was found, and the town emptied.

This is a stock certificate for the Ubehebe Copper Mines and Smelter Company, one of hundreds of mining companies formed in the Death Valley region between 1906 and 1908 to capitalize on the speculative frenzy caused by rising copper prices. Almost none of the mines produced anything, and investors lost millions of dollars.

The town of Leadfield, located in Titus Canyon, was founded as a result of a stock swindle by C.C. Julian of Los Angeles. Leadfield had a post office that operated from June 1926 until the end of that year. Its population was about 500.

Leadfield prospered in 1926 and had a hotel, restaurants, saloons, and a very short-lived newspaper. As people began to realize there was no economic substance to the mining claims and that a scam had been perpetrated, the investors and residents all left.

The Tonopah & Tidewater Railroad established Leeland as a station along its main route into Rhyolite. The station, located six miles from the town of Lee, provided a shipping point for supplies and ore. Leeland had a Wells Fargo office, a three-room station, and a population of 25. (FG.)

The Lee Gold Grotto Mining Co. was located in the Lee Mining District. The Tonopah & Tidewater Railroad established regular train service on October 15, 1907, enabling Lee to reach its zenith shortly thereafter. The town survived until 1914, the year the post office closed.

Chloride City was the name of the mining camp located in the Chloride Cliff Mining District, which is now in Death Valley National Park. The town was established in 1905, during the heyday of the Bullfrog mining excitement. It was built on the site of earlier mining activity in the 1870s.

96

Described as a "rare prize," this eight-hole outhouse has long vanished from the meager ruins that are left of Chloride City. If there is a lingering romance about the Old West and days gone by, perhaps this photograph will help put into perspective the hardships and deprivations the miners endured.

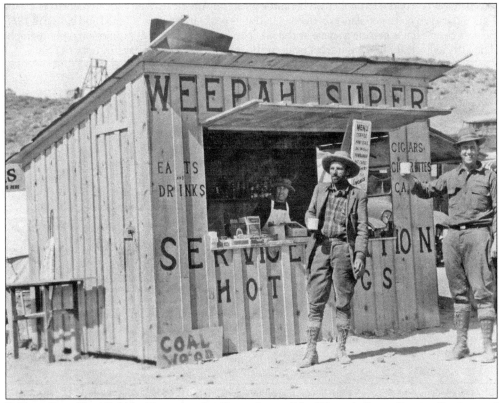

Seldom Seen Slim (left) holds a cup of coffee in front of the Weepah Super Service Station and Hot Dog Stand. Station owner E.H. Donegan is on the right, toasting Slim. This building was the first structure in Weepah.

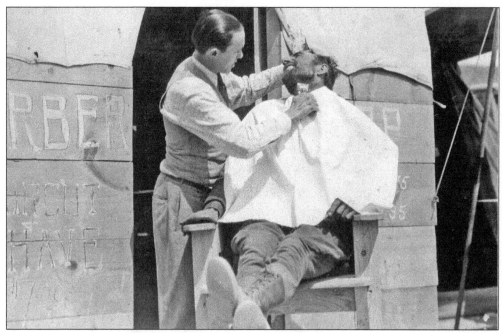

Weepah was one of the last gold rush boomtowns in the American West. Located north of Death Valley, the town had a population of about 2,000 at its peak, and it both boomed and busted in 1927. Seldom Seen Slim is getting a shave at the Weepah barbershop in this promotional photograph. The US Geological Survey named a peak in the Panamints "Slim's Peak" in honor of Slim.

The Clock Tower at Scotty's Castle is covered in snow during construction. Originally, the castle was conceived as a two-story stucco house so that Death Valley Scotty's friend, Chicago insurance executive Albert Johnson, could bring his wife to Death Valley. The plans for the house kept changing, until construction of the Spanish-influenced mansion began in 1925.

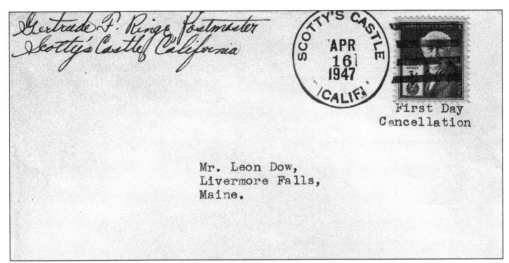

The number of visitors to Scotty's Castle was constantly increasing, and the post office opened an office there. This envelope was mailed in 1947, on the first day that the post office at Scotty's Castle was open. It was sent by Gertrude F. Ringe, the postmaster. The post office ceased operations on May 15, 1953.

This 1939 photograph is titled "Pair to Wed at Death Valley Scotty's Castle." Albert Johnson stands between Joseph Choate and Dorothy Drew, who were married at the castle. Death Valley Scotty was the best man, and Johnson gave the bride away. Nearly 100 guests, including a number of world-famous persons, had been invited to the affair.

SCOTTY'S CASTLE

Open All Year—Air Conditioned

Food service: Breakfast, Dinner, Snacks.

RESERVATION AND ACCOMMODATION INFORMATION

LODGING: Rooms and suites available in Hacienda and Rancho. European Plan.

HACIENDA:

	Single or Double	Three
MADRID ROOM Twin beds, tub and shower bath	$10	
GRANADA SUITE Large living room, bed divan, twin beds on balcony, lavatory	12	$15
BARCELONA SUITE Large living room, bed divan, twin beds on balcony, tub and shower bath	14	17
MAJORCA ROOM Twin beds, tub and shower bath	10	

RANCHO:

$6.00 single, or double. (Hot and cold water. Shower bath and other facilities nearby.)

$8.00 single, or double. (Hot and cold water. Shower bath en suite.)

When making reservations please include remittance to cover one day's charges. At least five days time should be allowed for confirmation from California points—other points accordingly.

Refund of deposits necessarily conditioned on receipt of notice of cancellation at head office 3 days or more in advance of anticipated arrival date.

Please make checks payable to "The Castle."

All communications and remittances may be mailed to head office: Scotty's Castle, 1462 No. Stanley Ave., Hollywood 46, California. Telephone: HOllywood 5-1223

The town of Scotty's Castle was an overnight tourist destination, as is evidenced by this advertising brochure and price list. There were a variety of rooms available in all price ranges, as well as other amenities. Note that there is air-conditioning, and all meals were available at the restaurant.

This photograph of the Scotty's Castle complex provides an overview of most of the buildings needed for the small "town." Prominent features include the clock tower (far left), the castle itself (right of center), the unfinished swimming pool (left foreground), motel rooms for tourists (right), and gasoline pumps (foreground).

This dugout near Stovepipe Wells is said to be the remains of a stage stop on the road between Rhyolite and Skidoo in the early 1900s, used as a refreshment stand. It is often referred to as the "First Stove Pipe Wells Hotel." This photograph was taken in the late 1920s, as the dugout began to slowly melt into the desert.

George Cook is shown standing in front of the store at Stove Pipe Springs in January 1907. The store is in a tent building marked "Grocery, Hay and Grain, Cigars, Tobacco, Meals." On the back of this photograph is written "This was the original Stove Pipe Wells Hotel." When this photograph was taken, Cook was on his way back to Skidoo.

This photograph of "Bungalette City" was taken in 1926. On some maps of Death Valley printed in the 1920s, there is a town called Bungalette City located between Darwin and Furnace Creek, at the end of the Eichbaum toll road. Bungalette City was actually the short-lived original name of what is now Stovepipe Wells.

Sand Spring was located about eight miles north of the extreme northwest corner of Death Valley. By 1927, after this photograph was taken, it boasted a gas station and store to service nearby Skookum. The cabin in this photograph was built by a homesteader.

Six

SKIDOO, RYAN, AND POINTS SOUTH

Very little is left of the town of Skidoo, which is today best remembered for two things: its unusual name and the vigilante hanging of Joe "Hootch" Simpson for the murder of Jim Arnold. Though there is much speculation about how Skidoo got its name, the one most accepted by scholars is that, in 1906, when Bob Montgomery purchased 23 claims in the area, his wife exclaimed "23 Skidoo," which was a popular expression at the time.

Originally called Amargosa, Death Valley Junction was established where the Tonopah & Tidewater Railroad connected to a branch line that went to the Pacific Coast Borax Company's borax deposits at Ryan. Its post office opened in 1908, and the town consisted of a saloon, a dozen houses, a store, and a restaurant. When mining operations stopped at Ryan, the town reinvented itself as a gateway to Death Valley. Its civic center was converted into the Amargosa Hotel. Today, the Death Valley Junction Historic District is in the National Register of Historic Places.

Francis Marion "Borax Smith" obtained the Lila C mining properties from William Coleman and started the first borax operations there in 1907. He began production a few months before the Tonopah & Tidewater Railroad reached the mine; mule teams transported the ore until the arrival of the railroad. The name was also changed to Ryan at that time, in honor of John Ryan, the general superintendent of the Tonopah & Tidewater Railroad. The Ryan Post Office was opened in 1907, and it transferred to (new) Ryan in 1914, when the Lila C became known as "Old Ryan."

Other towns on the Tonopah & Tidewater Railroad that are now ghosts include Dumont, Evelyn, Gerstley, Jenifer, Rasor, Valjean, and Zabriskie. All of these towns were named for railroad executives, except for Evelyn, which was named by Borax Smith for his wife. Ryan was another town named for a railroad executive, John Ryan, though its existence was owed to borax mining and the Lila C mine, and should not be considered a railroad town as such.

Skidoo was another Death Valley mining town that came into existence in 1906. It lasted until 1917, longer than most of the others. Bob Montgomery, the founder of Rhyolite, was the driving force behind Skidoo. Unlike many of the other Death Valley boomtowns, Skidoo did produce mining revenue, about $1.5 million. At its peak, Skidoo had a population of about 700, with a post office, a newspaper, and a telegraph.

In May 1908, the Skidoo mill started operation, and in early June, the first gold brick, worth $4,000, was sent to Rhyolite. Wells Fargo was then was responsible for its delivery to the US Mint. The mill had 10 stamps in operation and was handling about 35 tons of ore per day.

This stock certificate is for shares in the Skidoo Townsite and Mining Company. The company was formed on April 10, 1907, to raise money to develop the town and to profit the promoters. Matt Hoveck signed the certificate and served as the company's president.

This photograph of Skidoo was taken in 1907. Today, all that can be seen are a couple of foundations and traces of the main road that went through the town. Bob Montgomery originally named the town "23 Skidoo" from the popular expression of the day.

Like many mining camps, Skidoo boasted two baseball teams—the mine team and the town team. Here, both Skidoo baseball teams pose next to the Skidoo Dance Hall after having played a rivalry game on Independence Day in 1907. On the white uniforms, "23 BBC" stands for 23 [Skidoo] Baseball Club. On the left, George Cook is moving a piano over to this hall for the dance that night. (NPS.)

Cy K. Babcock, wearing a holstered gun, stands in the doorway of Skidoo Mines Company's headquarters administration building in 1931. The company was the largest employer in Skidoo, using up to 70 men when working at full capacity. Babcock operated the Wildrose Station and liked to be called "The Wildrose Kid."

Jim Arnold (right) operated the Skidoo Trading Company store and is considered to be one of its founders. He was the original locator of the Skidoo townsite. Joe Gundy is the man on the left. Arnold was subsequently shot and killed by Joe "Hootch" Simpson in Skidoo's most celebrated crime.

On April 19, 1908, Joe "Hootch" Simpson, drunk as usual, tried to hold up Jim Arnold's store. But two customers stopped him, and Arnold unceremoniously kicked him out. Simpson was humiliated; later that afternoon, he shot and killed Arnold. His continual boasting of the shooting annoyed Arnold's friends, who ultimately broke into the jail holding Simpson and lynched him from a telephone pole.

"Hooch" Simpson
Skidoo, Calif.
Easter Sunday
1909

SKIDOO NEWS

II, NO 18   SKIDOO, INYO COUNTY, CALIFORNIA, SATURDAY, APRIL 25, 1908

MURDER IN CAMP
Murderer Lynched
WITH GENERAL APPROVAL

Simpson Shoots Jim Arnold Dead and Is Hanged By Citizens

disturbance which has shaken this community to the roots, past few days, opened on Sunday morning last, at about 'clock, when Joe Simpson, familiarly known as Joe 'Hootch' ing his favorite beverage) held up the Southern Calif. re, for the nimble sum of twenty dollars, that being the

raised his gun and shot Arn just below the heart. Turning quickly, he threw his gun on Mr. Dobbs behind the bank counter and commanded him to come out and die, but before he could fulfil his threat, he realized his own danger, and backed out into the street. Simpson's entrance to the store and the crack of the shot, caused a scene, that, for a moment, was more dramatically

Sellers should be highly commended for the great bravery he displayed through out the action. He virtually carried his life in his hand, from the time he appeared upon the street, until he had subdued the murderer. He showed great patience too, with McBain. Many officers would have shot him down without argument.

Simpson handcuffed, but jubilant at his cowardly crime and at the hot fight he had put up, was taken to the Club saloon, until a guard-house could be decided upon.

tions about his interference, that as nearly resulted in other deaths. After due deliberation, the jury, consisting o W. B. Follambee, M. Gaveland, A. H Swinerton, J. H. Wilson, C. J. Bassett A. T. Hall, J. J. Sheehy, F. Pflager and W. McCoy, brought in a verdict "that the deceased, James Arnold, had died from the effects of a gun-shot wound inflicted by Joseph L. Simpson."

Early in the day, the District Attorney was telegraphed for to take charge of the case. The funeral was arranged for the following day and it was then the widespread feeling of regret and

At the end of 1906, Skidoo was able to boast that it had its own newspaper, the *Skidoo News*, which published its first issue on December 21, 1906. By far, its most popular issue was that of April 25, 1908, which gave the account of the murder of Jim Arnold by Hootch Simpson and Simpson's subsequent lynching. The newspaper printed its last issue in August 1908.

In August 1908, Thomas Floss perished in Death Valley with his friend Emory Bodge. This photograph of Tommy Floss was taken by the party that left Skidoo to retrieve the bodies of Bodge and Floss, who foolishly decided to walk to Skidoo from Rhyolite in the middle of August.

Written on the back of this photograph is "Shorty Harris's Camp," and it is captioned "Harrisburg Camp, May 1908." However, it was not just Shorty Harris's camp. Shorty was the codiscoverer, with Jean Pierre "Pete" Aguereberry. The town's original name was to be Harrisberry.

Matt Hoveck was the general manager of Bob Montgomery's Skidoo Mines Company. He also served as president of the Skidoo Townsite Company. When the town of Skidoo was granted a post office in 1906, the postal service originally named it Hoveck rather than Montgomery (Bob Montgomery's choice) or Skidoo (thought to be too slang). Ultimately, the town was renamed Skidoo in 1907.

Carl Glasscock is at a Wood Canyon prospector's camp, overseeing the pipeline that had finally been completed by the beginning of 1908. The pipeline, also known as the Telescope Peak Pipeline, was an ambitious project by E.A. "Bob" Montgomery to bring much-needed water from Birch Spring, just north of Telescope Peak, into Skidoo for mining and milling purposes.

Death Valley Junction was at the confluence of the Death Valley Railroad and the Tonopah & Tidewater Railroad. This photograph shows the town in 1935. By 1943, the railroad would completely stop serving the town, leading to its ultimate desertion. However, in 1967, dancer Marta Beckett took over the town, and she operated the Amargosa Opera House until 2012.

The town of Death Valley Junction is seen here in 1919. The works of the Pacific Coast Borax Company are at left. At right, employee housing lines the street leading to the rest of the town.

The town of Jenifer was located 18 miles north of Death Valley Junction. Named for railroad executive Frank M. Jenifer, it was little more than a spur of the Tonopah & Tidewater Railroad, of which nothing remains. Frank Jenifer's business card as an assistant traffic agent predates his being named president of the Death Valley Railroad. He conceived the idea for building the Furnace Creek Inn in 1925.

The road leading to Furnace Creek Ranch is clearly visible about 20 years after the 1912 photograph on the next page was taken. More buildings and palm trees are in evidence. Today, Furnace Creek Ranch is the name of the tourist complex near the Furnace Creek Inn. The Timbisha Shoshone still maintain a tribal village area near Furnace Creek Ranch. (Willard.)

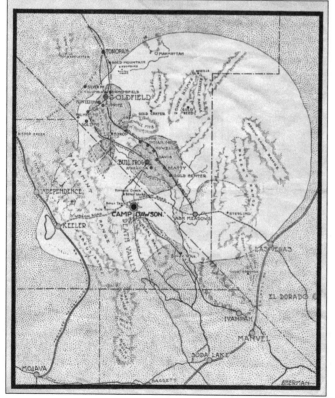

This skull-shaped map was made by B.X. Dawson for as a promotion for "Camp Dawson," a fictional mining camp south of Furnace Creek in Death Valley. The map was created to fleece investors during the mining boom of 1905–1906. Dawson claimed to have found prehistoric mining tools in the area, and he formed the Death Valley Gold Mining & Milling Company to capitalize on it.

This photograph of Furnace Creek Ranch was taken in 1912. Furnace Creek Ranch, originally known as Greenland Ranch, was started by the Pacific Coast Borax Company at the mouth of Furnace Creek in the mid-1880s. The highest temperature ever recorded on Earth was made near this site in July 1913.

Bill Keyes shows off the mechanical man he made at China Ranch in 1911. Keys Camp was located just east of Zabriskie on the Tonopah & Tidewater route map (see page 2). Keyes was an early Death Valley prospector. An ally of Death Valley Scotty, Keyes provided Scotty with the use of his mines to give credence to Scotty's claims to prospective investors. Keyes's name is often misspelled as "Keys."

The Argenta mining camp in Death Valley was located near Aguereberry Point. In 1908, Dan Driscoll filed the first claim, although there are conflicting reports of ownership. In any event, George C. Griest took over ownership in 1929 or 1930 and was living there in 1933. Griest, known as "Sheriff of the Panamints," owned it until 1968. The Argenta mine produced lead, silver, and zinc.

The town of Ryan was originally located at the Lila C mine, about seven miles southwest of Death Valley Junction. About 1915, the Lila C ore deposits were running out, and the buildings were moved to the Biddy McCarthy deposit, about 12 miles to the northwest. Originally named Devar, the post office did not agree with the name and reinstated the Ryan name for this new town.

Mr. Montgomery and his wife, "Monty," sit on the porch of their house at Ryan. Mr. Montgomery is holding a folding Kodak camera and appears to be using a crutch, possibly for an injury resulting from a mining accident, an all-too-common occurrence. "Monty" Montgomery is holding a kitten. Cats were highly prized pets, used to control the mice and rat population.

The Widow Train was the Ryan narrow-gauge railroad used to transport borax. It was named for the Widow mine near Ryan. This photograph is unusual, as it shows the train being used for its original purpose, transporting borax. After the mines closed, the train was modified to carry tourists.

In 1928, the "baby-gauge" railroad that formerly carried borax from the mines near Ryan was converted to carry passengers to the Death Valley View Hotel, which previously housed the mine employees. Open-air cars transported the visitors on trestles, through tunnels, along the mountains, and inside mines. Later, it became a stand-alone tourist attraction.

Margaret "Betty" Boyd is standing next to a firebox in Ryan. Fire was always a problem in frontier towns, and especially so in hot, dry, desert areas such as Death Valley. These boxes were strategically placed around Ryan to provide a source of water, buckets, and hoses in the event of fire.

"Monty" Montgomery holds Billie Potts around 1921. In the background are the new bunkhouses, shower house, and boiler house. The view is to the northeast. This is the only known photograph of the shower house that served the dormitories for the miners and their families. The shower house is located in "new Ryan."

Ryan had both men's and women's baseball teams. On occasion, they played against teams from Death Valley Junction, Shoshone, and Beatty. Ryan's topography was too steep to allow anyone to play baseball, so people went to the Travertine Springs area for ball games, picnics, and socializing.

This 1924 photograph shows a group of Ryan children at a birthday party. The two-story building in the left foreground is a bunkhouse. The building in the background on the far left was the old superintendent's house, later turned into the hospital, and finally converted to guest housing for the Death Valley View Hotel. To the right is a staff house known today as House 3.

The schoolhouse at Ryan was built about 1922, shortly before this photograph was taken. The one-room schoolhouse accommodated all grades and had an outhouse in the back. The eight children shown here would have been the entire student population.

The swimming pool and recreational grounds for the mine employees and their families at Ryan were located at Travertine Springs, at the headwaters of Furnace Creek. Note the changing shed roofed with palm fronds. These springs were also the source for a later swimming pool, built to serve the upscale Furnace Creek Inn.

The town of Kasson, located southwest of Tecopa, was founded in 1879 by Amasa C. Kasson and John S. Thompson. The Gladstone Gold & Silver Mining Company was the economic engine for the town. Kasson was awarded a post office in July 1879, when its application claimed a population of 75. However, once it was determined no one lived within 25 miles, the post office was discontinued.

"Devil's Bake Oven in Amargosa, California" is the caption for this photograph. Indian burial grounds are seen in the immediate foreground, and the mining camp is in the background. The mining camp was probably located near where the Amargosa Borax Works operated south of Shoshone in the 1880s. There was a short-lived town, Amargosa, near Rhyolite. All of its buildings were moved to Bullfrog.

The town of Groom was located east of Death Valley, at the junction of Emigrant and Death Valleys. Some authors believe that the presence of Spanish bayonet plants in this photograph (circled, in the foreground, left of center) proves that Sheldon Young and the "Jayhawkers" passed through here on December 2, 1849. Sheldon Young was a member of the original party of the group of pioneers that crossed Death Valley in 1849. There was a disagreement over the best route to take across Death Valley and the party split into three separate groups, each taking its own route. Young was in the Jayhawkers (the other two groups were the "Georgians" and the "Mississippi Boys"), and he kept the only contemporaneous record on the journey to California. Young's record is used by historians to try determine the route the Jayhawkers took across Death Valley, a point of considerable debate. On December 2, 1849, Young noted that he saw a Spanish bayonet. The photograph illustrates the only place in all of the possible routes where a Spanish bayonet was found, hence its importance in determining the route the Jayhawkers took.

This washout occurred at Evelyn in 1908. Named for Evelyn Ellis, Borax Smith's second wife, the town of Evelyn was built in 1907. It was basically a siding on the Tonopah & Tidewater Railroad. It consisted of living quarters and housing as well as tool facilities. In 1943, the section house in Evelyn was moved to Shoshone.

The caption "Colemanite" on this photograph may refer either to the mineral Colemanite, which is the whitish substance that can be seen in the foreground, or to the Colemanite station, located near Ryan on the Death Valley Railroad, seen far in the background. Both the mineral and the town were named for borax man William Tell Coleman.

The town of Johnnie was located east of Death Valley Junction. It grew up around and was named for the Johnnie mine, located a few miles northeast of the townsite. By 1907, Johnnie had a population of 350 people, with saloons, stores, and restaurants. The Johnnie Mill is shown in this photograph.

The Johnnie Greenwater Consolidated Copper Company was named to take advantage of the relationship between the Tonopah & Tidewater Railroad siding at Johnnie and the copper mines at Greenwater, 55 miles away. Although the company had 23 claims over 46 acres, like all other Greenwater mines, it was a promotional scam and never produced.

Famed prospector John Lemoigne's Mine Camp was at the north end of the Panamint Mountains, in Cottonwood Canyon. Lemoigne also discovered lead in Moigne Canyon, northwest of Emigrant Springs. While the exact location of this camp remains in dispute, in 1897, Lemoigne's property was mentioned as one incentive for construction of a railroad route to develop the mineral resources in the Panamint Valley area.

The town Carbonate sprang up as a result of the mining interests in the Carbonate Lead Mines Company, located a little south of Galena Canyon in Death Valley. An unidentified man is standing in the doorway of a makeshift wooden structure built into the side of a hill, identified as the camp kitchen at Carbonate.

Christian B. Zabriskie is the man standing next to a fully loaded burro between two unidentified prospectors in this 1904 photograph. Most visitors to Death Valley are familiar with Zabriskie Point, but few are aware of the now ghost town of Zabriskie, which was a stop on the Tonopah & Tidewater Railroad. Both are named for Christian B. Zabriskie.

This Bullfrog Goldfield Railroad Company receipt was for a shipment being sent to Chester Pray in the town of Zabriskie. In 1908, Chester A. Pray discovered the Carbonate, a lead mine in Death Valley. Pray developed the mine with Jack Salsberry and formed Carbonate Lead Mines. In June 1913, shortly after this shipment, Pray committed suicide by shooting himself in the head.

The town of Russell's Camp was located two miles west of Ryan. W. Scott Russell staked some borax claims in Furnace Creek Wash; when he went to record them, he found out that United States Borax never perfected its title to the most profitable claim. Russell subsequently restaked it and obtained legal title. It was the subject of a number of lawsuits, but Russell ultimately prevailed.

The ghost town of Ibex is located at the southeastern end of Death Valley. In the 1880s, it had a mine, mill, and smelter. In 1907, it emerged as a mining camp for silver mines. Bob Montgomery (left), Sam Yount, and Mr. Shattuck (right) are shown in Ibex Wash. Bob Montgomery is best known as the discoverer of the Montgomery Shoshone mine in Rhyolite and the Oh Be Joyful mine in Ballarat.

Wildrose Station had tourist cabins, a store, eating facilities, and a gas station. Earlier, Wildrose Station served as a stage station on the Ballarat-Skidoo road and had been a stop for prospectors since the 1870s. There have been no commercial enterprises at Wildrose since 1972, when the US Park Service deemed it unsafe for tourism and most of the structures were removed. Wildrose station is located about 27 miles north of Ballarat.

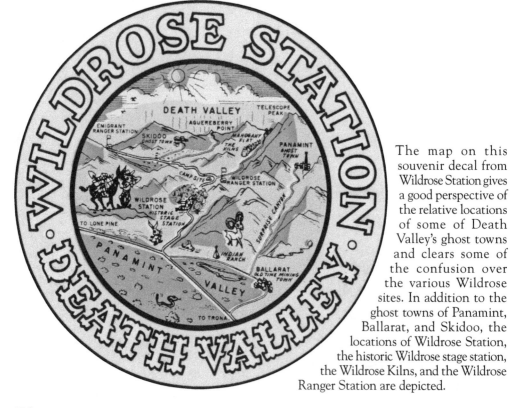

The map on this souvenir decal from Wildrose Station gives a good perspective of the relative locations of some of Death Valley's ghost towns and clears some of the confusion over the various Wildrose sites. In addition to the ghost towns of Panamint, Ballarat, and Skidoo, the locations of Wildrose Station, the historic Wildrose stage station, the Wildrose Kilns, and the Wildrose Ranger Station are depicted.

BIBLIOGRAPHY

Chalfant, W.A. *The Story of Inyo*. Revised edition. Bishop, CA: Chalfant Press, 1933.

Cragan, Dorothy Clora. *The Boys in the Sky-Blue Pants*. Independence, CA: Pioneer Publishing Company, 1975.

Green, Linda W., and John A. Latschar. *Historic Resource Study: A History of Mining in Death Valley National Monument*. Denver: National Park Service, 1981.

Hubbard, Paul B., Doris Bray, and George Pipkin. *Ballarat Facts and Folklore*. Lancaster, CA: Privately published, 1965.

Johnston, Hank. *Death Valley Scotty: "The Fastest Con in the West"*. Corona del Mar, CA: Trans-Anglo Books, 1974.

Lingenfelter, Richard E. *Death Valley & The Amargosa*. Berkeley: University of California Press, 1986.

Myrick, David F. *Railroads of Nevada and Eastern California*. Berkeley: Howell-North Books, 1963.

Palazzo, Robert P. *Darwin, California*. Lake Grove, OR: Western Places, 1996.

———. *Post Offices and Postmasters of Inyo County, California 1866–1966*. Fernley, NV: Doug MacDonald, 2005.

Visit us at
arcadiapublishing.com

....

Printed in the USA
CPSIA information can be obtained
at www.ICGtesting.com
LVHW081957171123
764248LV00009B/839